CRIMINAL JUSTICE, LAW ENFORCEMENT AND CORRECTIONS

THE FEDERAL BUREAU OF PRISONS' COMPASSIONATE RELEASE PROGRAM

CRIMINAL JUSTICE, LAW ENFORCEMENT AND CORRECTIONS

CRIMINAL JUSTICE, LAW ENFORCEMENT AND CORRECTIONS

THE FEDERAL BUREAU OF PRISONS' COMPASSIONATE RELEASE PROGRAM

JOSIAH N. MARLEINS
EDITOR

nova publishers
New York

For permission to use material from this book please contact us:
Telephone 631-231-7269; Fax 631-231-8175
Web Site: http://www.novapublishers.com

Library of Congress Cataloging-in-Publication Data

ISBN 978-1-62808-318-7

Published by Nova Science Publishers, Inc. † New York

CONTENTS

PREFACE

In the Sentencing Reform Act of 1984, Congress authorized the Director of the Federal Bureau of Prisons (BOP) to request that a federal judge reduce an inmate's sentence for "extraordinary and compelling" circumstances. Under the statute, the request can be based on either medical or non-medical conditions that could not reasonably have been foreseen by the judge at the time of sentencing. The BOP has issued regulations and a Program Statement entitled "compassionate release" to implement this authority. The Office of the Inspector General (OIG) found that an effectively managed compassionate release program would result in cost savings for the BOP, as well as assist the BOP in managing its continually growing inmate population and the significant capacity challenges it is facing. However, the existing BOP compassionate release program has been poorly managed and implemented inconsistently, likely resulting in eligible inmates not being considered for release and in terminally ill inmates dying before their requests were decided. This book assesses the BOP's compassionate release program, including whether it provides cost savings or other benefits to the BOP.

Chapter 1 - In the *Sentencing Reform Act of 1984*, Congress authorized the Director of the Federal Bureau of Prisons (BOP) to request that a federal judge reduce an inmate's sentence for "extraordinary and compelling" circumstances. Under the statute, the request can be based on either medical or non-medical conditions that could not reasonably have been foreseen by the judge at the time of sentencing.

The BOP has issued regulations and a Program Statement entitled "compassionate release" to implement this authority. This review assessed the BOP's compassionate release program, including whether it provides cost savings or other benefits to the BOP.

Results in Brief

The Office of the Inspector General (OIG) found that an effectively managed compassionate release program would result in cost savings for the BOP, as well as assist the BOP in managing its continually growing inmate population and the significant capacity challenges it is facing. However, the authors found that the existing BOP compassionate release program has been poorly managed and implemented inconsistently, likely resulting in eligible inmates not being considered for release and in terminally ill inmates dying before their requests were decided.

The BOP does not have clear standards on when compassionate release is warranted, resulting in ad hoc decision making. The BOP's regulations and Program Statement provide no criteria or standards to use in evaluating whether a medical or nonmedical circumstance qualifies for consideration. As a result, the authors found that BOP staff had varied and inconsistent understandings of the circumstances that warranted consideration for compassionate release. For example, at some institutions, only inmates with a life expectancy of 6 months or less were deemed eligible for consideration. At other institutions, inmates with a life expectancy of 12 months or less were considered eligible candidates. The authors further found that although the BOP's regulations and Program Statement permit non-medical circumstances to be considered as a basis for compassionate release, the BOP routinely rejects such requests and did not approve a single non-medical request during the 6-year period of their review.

ODAG and BOP officials told us that the BOP is currently revising its compassionate release regulations and, subsequently, the compassionate release Program Statement. In addition, the BOP is drafting a new guidance memorandum for medical institutions that will expand the compassionate release program by making inmates with a life expectancy of up to 18 months eligible for consideration and assist staff who review compassionate release requests in understanding what level of functioning is sufficiently "extraordinary and compelling" for inmates with debilitating medical conditions to be considered for release. However, the BOP did not provide the OIG with a copy of the memorandum under consideration and could not tell us when it would be finalized.

The BOP does not have formal timeliness standards for reviewing requests, and timeliness standards for inmate appeals do not consider the special circumstances of medical compassionate release requests. Although many inmates eligible for compassionate release have terminal illnesses and limited life expectancies, the Program Statement simply directs staff to "expedite" the review process. The authors found that not all institutions have timeliness standards, and for those institutions that do, the timeframe ranges from 5 to 65 days. In addition, the process available to inmates to appeal a Warden's or Regional Director's denial of a compassionate release request can take up to more than 5 months to complete.

The BOP does not have effective procedures to inform inmates about the program. The compassionate release program is not one of the BOP programs that staff is required to inform inmates about. As a result, the authors found that the means used to inform inmates about the program are informal and vary by institution. The authors also reviewed handbooks provided to inmates upon arriving at an institution and found that only 8 of the 111 handbooks had information regarding compassionate release.

The BOP does not have a system to track all requests, the timeliness of the review process, or whether decisions made by Wardens and Regional Directors are consistent with each other or with BOP policy. The BOP cannot account for all compassionate release requests processed at its institutions from 2006 through 2011 because it tracks requests only in two situations: first, when a request has been approved by both a Warden and a Regional Director and has been sent to the BOP Director for consideration, and second, when an inmate has appealed a Warden's or Regional Director's decision denying a request.

The authors also found that the BOP cannot determine if requests are processed in a timely manner because the BOP does not track the time it takes to approve or deny requests. As a result, the BOP cannot determine if delays in the process exist, take corrective actions where delays occur, or ensure that inmates who may be eligible for the program, particularly those with terminal illnesses, are considered for release in a timely manner. According to case files provided by the BOP, in 13 percent (28 of 208) of the cases where inmate requests had been approved by a Warden and Regional Director, the inmate died before a final decision was made by the BOP Director.

In addition, the authors found that the BOP does not conduct any systematic reviews of decisions made by Wardens or Regional Directors to ensure that they are consistent with each other and with the BOP's Program Statement and the underlying statutory authority. As a result, the BOP cannot ensure the appropriateness of denial decisions made by Wardens or Regional Directors.

The release of inmates through the compassionate release program provides cost savings for the BOP and assists the BOP with prison

population management. The authors found that a properly managed compassionate release program inevitably provides cost savings to the BOP and provides assistance to the BOP in addressing its ever-increasing and significant capacity problems. However, the authors also found that the BOP does not maintain cost data associated with the custody of inmates eligible for consideration under the program, and the authors found that the BOP has conducted no analysis of cost savings achieved by releasing such inmates. As a result, neither the BOP nor the OIG can determine with any precision the costs associated with providing health care to inmates eligible for compassionate release or the cost savings achieved by releasing eligible inmates.

A small percentage of inmates were rearrested after being released under the compassionate release program. In considering the impact of the compassionate release program on public safety, the authors found a recidivism rate of 3.5 percent for inmates released through the program. By comparison, the general recidivism rate for federal prisoners has been estimated to be as high as 41 percent. The OIG recognizes that approving and releasing more eligible inmates through the compassionate release program could result in some increase in the number of inmates who are rearrested. But the recidivism data the authors found demonstrates that a carefully and effectively managed program can minimize that risk if careful consideration is given to an inmate's potential risk to the community as part of the assessment process.

Recommendations

In this report, the authors make 11 recommendations to improve the BOP's management of the compassionate release program and to ensure that eligible inmates are considered for release. These recommendations include considering appropriately expanding the use of the compassionate release program as authorized by Congress and as described in the BOP's regulations and Program Statement to cover both medical and non-medical conditions for inmates who do not present a threat to the community and who present a minimal risk of recidivism, updating written national policies to accurately reflect the BOP's criteria for determining eligible medical and non-medical requests, and establishing timeframes for processing requests at each step of the review process. The authors also recommend the BOP require that all inmates be informed about the compassionate release program and that the

BOP track each compassionate release request, its status, and final disposition. The authors also recommend that the BOP collect and assess the costs for providing health services to inmates diagnosed with terminal medical conditions and a limited life expectancy, and severely debilitating medical conditions.

Chapter 2 - This report provides an update to annual tables based on the Bureau of Justice Statistics' (BJS) Deaths in Custody Reporting Program (DCRP), a data collection that measures inmate mortality data in state prisons and local jails by the number and causes of deaths. In 2008, 960 inmates died in U.S. jails (a mortality rate of 123 deaths per 100,000 jail inmates). In 2009, 948 inmates died in U.S. jails (a rate of 127 deaths per 100,000 jail inmates). State prison facilities reported 3,452 inmate deaths in 2008 (a rate of 260 deaths per 100,000 prison inmates) and 3,408 inmate deaths in 2009 (257 deaths per 100,000 prison inmates). Consistent with data from previous years, local jail deaths constituted approximately 25% of inmate deaths in adult correctional facilities nationwide.

The number of inmate deaths in jails increased each year between 2000 and 2007 (from 904 to 1,102 inmate deaths), increasing 22% during this period. In 2008, the number of deaths in jails declined 13% to 960 inmate deaths, and decreased an additional 1% in 2009 to 948 deaths. The decline in 2008 was the first decline in jail mortality data since BJS began collecting data annually for the DCRP in 2000.

From 2007 to 2008, 918 jails reported a change in the number of deaths to the DCRP. Among these jails, 324 reported a total increase of 452 deaths and 402 jails reported a total decrease of 594 deaths, for a net decrease of 142 deaths in 2008. The majority of jails reporting a decline (74%) registered one less death in 2008 than in 2007. Nine jails reported a total decrease of 69 deaths (12% of the total decline). All nine of these jails held at least 2,500 inmates on an average day in 2007 and 2008.

In general, the number of deaths in state prisons rose each year between 2001 and 2008 (from 2,877 to 3,452 inmate deaths), a 20% increase. In 2009, the number of deaths in prisons dropped to 3,408, a 1% decrease.

Statistical tables in this report detail prison and jail deaths in custody. The tables present mortality data by cause of death, selected decedent characteristics, and state.

In: The Federal Bureau of Prisons' … ISBN 978-1-62808-318-7
Editor: Josiah N. Marleins

Chapter 1

THE FEDERAL BUREAU OF PRISONS' COMPASSIONATE RELEASE PROGRAM*

U.S. Department of Justice,
Office of the Inspector General

EXECUTIVE DIGEST

In the *Sentencing Reform Act of 1984*, Congress authorized the Director of the Federal Bureau of Prisons (BOP) to request that a federal judge reduce an inmate's sentence for "extraordinary and compelling" circumstances.[1] Under the statute, the request can be based on either medical or non-medical conditions that could not reasonably have been foreseen by the judge at the time of sentencing.[2]

The BOP has issued regulations and a Program Statement entitled "compassionate release" to implement this authority.[3] This review assessed the BOP's compassionate release program, including whether it provides cost savings or other benefits to the BOP.

* This report, I-2013-006, was released April 2013 by the U.S. Department of Justice, Office of the Inspector General, Evaluation and Inspections Division.

Results in Brief

The Office of the Inspector General (OIG) found that an effectively managed compassionate release program would result in cost savings for the BOP, as well as assist the BOP in managing its continually growing inmate population and the significant capacity challenges it is facing. However, we found that the existing BOP compassionate release program has been poorly managed and implemented inconsistently, likely resulting in eligible inmates not being considered for release and in terminally ill inmates dying before their requests were decided.

The BOP does not have clear standards on when compassionate release is warranted, resulting in ad hoc decision making. The BOP's regulations and Program Statement provide no criteria or standards to use in evaluating whether a medical or nonmedical circumstance qualifies for consideration. As a result, we found that BOP staff had varied and inconsistent understandings of the circumstances that warranted consideration for compassionate release. For example, at some institutions, only inmates with a life expectancy of 6 months or less were deemed eligible for consideration. At other institutions, inmates with a life expectancy of 12 months or less were considered eligible candidates. We further found that although the BOP's regulations and Program Statement permit non-medical circumstances to be considered as a basis for compassionate release, the BOP routinely rejects such requests and did not approve a single nonmedical request during the 6-year period of our review.

ODAG and BOP officials told us that the BOP is currently revising its compassionate release regulations and, subsequently, the compassionate release Program Statement. In addition, the BOP is drafting a new guidance memorandum for medical institutions that will expand the compassionate release program by making inmates with a life expectancy of up to 18 months eligible for consideration and assist staff who review compassionate release requests in understanding what level of functioning is sufficiently "extraordinary and compelling" for inmates with debilitating medical conditions to be considered for release. However, the BOP did not provide the OIG with a copy of the memorandum under consideration and could not tell us when it would be finalized.

The BOP does not have formal timeliness standards for reviewing requests, and timeliness standards for inmate appeals do not consider the special circumstances of medical compassionate release requests. Although many inmates eligible for compassionate release have terminal illnesses and limited life expectancies, the Program Statement simply directs staff to "expedite" the review process. We found that not all institutions have timeliness standards, and for those institutions that do, the timeframe ranges from 5 to 65 days. In addition, the process available to inmates to appeal a Warden's or Regional Director's denial of a compassionate release request can take up to more than 5 months to complete.

The BOP does not have effective procedures to inform inmates about the program. The compassionate release program is not one of the BOP programs that staff is required to inform inmates about. As a result, we found that the means used to inform inmates about the program are informal and vary by institution. We also reviewed handbooks provided to inmates upon arriving at an institution and found that only 8 of the 111 handbooks had information regarding compassionate release.[4]

The BOP does not have a system to track all requests, the timeliness of the review process, or whether decisions made by Wardens and Regional Directors are consistent with each other or with BOP policy. The BOP cannot account for all compassionate release requests processed at its institutions from 2006 through 2011 because it tracks requests only in two situations: first, when a request has been approved by both a Warden and a Regional Director and has been sent to the BOP Director for consideration, and second, when an inmate has appealed a Warden's or Regional Director's decision denying a request.

We also found that the BOP cannot determine if requests are processed in a timely manner because the BOP does not track the time it takes to approve or deny requests. As a result, the BOP cannot determine if delays in the process exist, take corrective actions where delays occur, or ensure that inmates who may be eligible for the program, particularly those with terminal illnesses, are considered for release in a timely manner. According to case files provided by the BOP, in 13 percent (28 of 208) of the cases where inmate requests had been approved by a Warden and Regional Director, the inmate died before a final decision was made by the BOP Director.

In addition, we found that the BOP does not conduct any systematic reviews of decisions made by Wardens or Regional Directors to ensure that they are consistent with each other and with the BOP's Program Statement and the underlying statutory authority. As a result, the BOP cannot ensure the appropriateness of denial decisions made by Wardens or Regional Directors.

The release of inmates through the compassionate release program provides cost savings for the BOP and assists the BOP with prison population management. We found that a properly managed compassionate release program inevitably provides cost savings to the BOP and provides assistance to the BOP in addressing its ever-increasing and significant capacity problems.[5] However, we also found that the BOP does not maintain cost data associated with the custody of inmates eligible for consideration under the program, and we found that the BOP has conducted no analysis of cost savings achieved by releasing such inmates. As a result, neither the BOP nor the OIG can determine with any precision the costs associated with providing health care to inmates eligible for compassionate release or the cost savings achieved by releasing eligible inmates.

A small percentage of inmates were rearrested after being released under the compassionate release program. In considering the impact of the compassionate release program on public safety, we found a recidivism rate of 3.5 percent for inmates released through the program. By comparison, the general recidivism rate for federal prisoners has been estimated to be as high as 41 percent. The OIG recognizes that approving and releasing more eligible inmates through the compassionate release program could result in some increase in the number of inmates who are rearrested. But the recidivism data we found demonstrates that a carefully and effectively managed program can minimize that risk if careful consideration is given to an inmate's potential risk to the community as part of the assessment process.

Recommendations

In this report, we make 11 recommendations to improve the BOP's management of the compassionate release program and to ensure that eligible inmates are considered for release. These recommendations include considering appropriately expanding the use of the compassionate release program as authorized by Congress and as described in the BOP's regulations and Program Statement to cover both medical and non-medical conditions for inmates who do not present a threat to the community and who present a minimal risk of recidivism, updating written national policies to accurately reflect the BOP's criteria for determining eligible medical and non-medical requests, and establishing timeframes for processing requests at each step of the review process. We also recommend the BOP require that all inmates be informed about the compassionate release program and that the BOP track each compassionate release request, its status, and final disposition. We also recommend that the BOP collect and assess the costs for providing health services to inmates diagnosed with terminal medical conditions and a limited life expectancy, and severely debilitating medical conditions.

BACKGROUND

Introduction

In the *Sentencing Reform Act of 1984,* Congress authorized a federal court to reduce an inmate's sentence of imprisonment, upon a motion by the Director of the Federal Bureau of Prisons (BOP), if the court finds "extraordinary and compelling" circumstances exist that warrant a reduction and that the reduction "is consistent with applicable policy statements" of the U.S. Sentencing Commission.[6] However, absent a motion by the Director of the BOP, a federal judge has no authority to modify an inmate's sentence for "extraordinary and compelling" reasons.

In connection with this authority, the BOP has promulgated regulations and issued a Program Statement, both entitled "compassionate release," that outline procedures for an inmate to initiate a request seeking a reduction in sentence for "extraordinary and compelling" reasons and that outline the process by which the BOP will consider the request.[7] However, the regulations and the Program Statement do not define "compassionate release" or what constitutes an "extraordinary and compelling" circumstances.

The BOP is responsible for the custody and care of approximately 218,000 federal offenders who are housed in 117 BOP-operated facilities and in 15 privately managed or community-based facilities under contract with the BOP.[8] We found that, on average, only 24 inmates are released each year through the BOP's compassionate release program.[9]

The Office of the Inspector General (OIG) examined the BOP's implementation of the authority given to it by Congress and its process to approve or deny inmate requests for "extraordinary and compelling" reasons. Specifically, we examined the information the BOP provided about the program to inmates and the policies and procedures the BOP used to evaluate inmate requests, including any guidance or criteria the BOP used to determine which circumstances qualified as "extraordinary and compelling." We also reviewed the timeliness with which the BOP processed requests, as well as the costs associated with the custody of inmates who might be eligible for release due to "extraordinary and compelling" circumstances. Lastly, we assessed the recidivism rates of those inmates who had been approved and released through the compassionate release program.

In this background section, we discuss the Department components involved in the compassionate release program, the process by which they consider inmate requests for release, and the federal laws and regulations and Department policies governing the compassionate release process.

Department Components Involved in the Compassionate Release Program and the Review Process

The compassionate release program involves three Department components: the BOP, U.S. Attorneys' Offices (USAO), and the Office of the Deputy Attorney General (ODAG). This section briefly describes each component's role in the program and the compassionate release review process.

The Federal Bureau of Prisons

The BOP administers the compassionate release program in accordance with 18 U.S.C. § 4205(g) (repealed 1987) or § 3582(c)(1)(A) and 28 C.F.R. § 571.60-.64. Under these authorities, the BOP Director may request a reduction in an inmate's sentence based on "extraordinary and compelling" circumstances that were not known at the time of an inmate's sentencing. However, the BOP generally has exercised its authority only with inmates who are suffering from a life-threatening or terminal medical condition, or who are severely and permanently mentally or physically disabled.

U.S. Attorneys' Offices

The USAOs have two roles in the compassionate release review process. First, when the BOP is considering whether an inmate is eligible for compassionate release, the BOP seeks an opinion from the Assistant U.S. Attorney (AUSA) who prosecuted the inmate's case on the circumstances underlying the inmate's request. An AUSA may support or oppose the inmate's request when responding to the BOP. Second, if the BOP Director approves a compassionate release request, the BOP will contact the USAO in the district in which the inmate was sentenced to request that the USAO make a motion to the federal sentencing court on behalf of the BOP to reduce the term of the inmate's sentence.

The Office of the Deputy Attorney General

The ODAG reviews two types of inmate requests for compassionate release that have been approved by the BOP Director: those made for non-medical reasons and those from inmates who are severely and permanently mentally or physically debilitated but whose life expectancy is indeterminate or unknown. In those circumstances, if the BOP Director approves the request, the request is forwarded to the ODAG for its review and the ODAG can object or raise concerns with the BOP Director before the request receives final approval.

The Compassionate Release Program's Review Process

According to the BOP's Program Statement and 28 C.F.R. § 571.61-.63, the compassionate release program's review process begins when an inmate submits a request to the Warden. A request must include the extraordinary and compelling circumstances that the inmate believes merit consideration; a plan for where the inmate will reside if released; and how he or she will support him- or herself if released. If the basis for the inmate's request is due to the inmate's health, information about where the inmate will receive medical care and how it will be paid for must also be included.

The Warden reviews the request and, if denying it, informs the inmate, in writing, of the reasons for the denial. The inmate may file an appeal through the BOP's administrative remedy procedures.[10] If the Warden determines that the request warrants approval, the Warden refers the matter in writing with an approval recommendation to the Regional Director.

Upon receiving a request that a Warden has recommended for approval, the Regional Director conducts a review to determine if the request warrants approval.[11] If the Regional Director denies the request, the Regional Director informs the inmate of the reasons for denial, and the inmate may file an appeal through the BOP's administrative remedy procedures. If the Regional Director approves the request, the request with a written approval recommendation is referred to the BOP Office of General Counsel at the BOP's Central Office.[12]

Upon receiving the approved request from the Regional Director, the General Counsel solicits the opinion of either the BOP Medical Director, for medically based requests, or the BOP Assistant Director, Correctional Programs Division, for non-medical requests, as well as the opinion of the prosecuting AUSA.[13] The General Counsel then forwards the inmate's request with these opinions and the recommendation from the Warden and the

Regional Director to the BOP Director for final decision. While both the BOP's regulations and Program Statement give the General Counsel the authority to make a final determination to deny the inmate's request, we were told by BOP Central Office staff and officials that the General Counsel does not make any final decisions regarding inmate requests for compassionate release.[14]

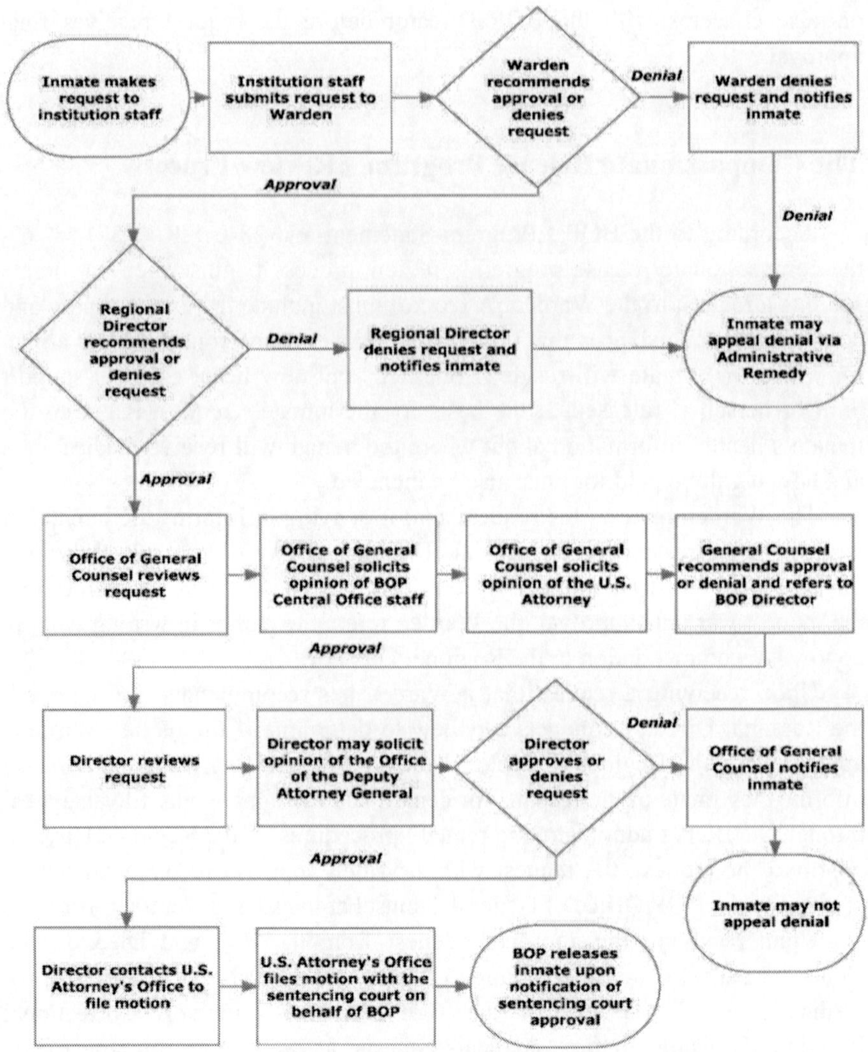

Source: BOP.

Figure 1. Compassionate Release Request and Review Process.

We learned if the inmate's request is based on non-medical reasons or upon a severely debilitating medical condition and the inmate has an indeterminate life expectancy, the BOP Director solicits the opinion of the ODAG before rendering a final decision. No provision in either the BOP regulations or Program Statement provides for or requires such a consultation.

If the BOP Director denies the inmate's request, the inmate must be informed of the reasons for the denial within 20 working days of the Warden receiving the denial from the General Counsel, and the denial constitutes a final administrative action that the inmate cannot appeal. If the BOP Director grants the request, the BOP Director requests that the USAO in the district in which the inmate was sentenced petition the sentencing court to reduce the inmate's term of imprisonment.[15] Figure 1 presents a flow chart illustrating the process.

Federal Laws, Regulations, and Guidelines, and Department Policies Related to Compassionate Release

Below is a summary of federal laws and regulations regarding compassionate release. Appendix I provides more descriptive information about the laws and regulations relevant to the compassionate release program.

Federal Statutes, Regulations, and Guidelines

Sentencing Reform Act of 1984 (Pub. L. No. 98-473, 18 U.S.C. §§ 3551-3556)

The *Sentencing Reform Act of 1984,* Title II of the *Comprehensive Crime Control Act of 1984,* was passed by Congress and signed into law by the President on October 12, 1984. The legislation permits an inmate to request that the BOP Director make a motion to the federal sentencing judge for a reduction in the inmate's sentence for "extraordinary and compelling" reasons.

Under 18 U.S.C. § 3582(c)(1)(A), a sentencing court, on motion of the BOP Director, may reduce the term of imprisonment of an inmate sentenced under the *Comprehensive Crime Control Act of 1984.* The BOP oversees this program in accordance with 18 U.S.C. § 3582(c)(1)(A) and the procedures set forth in 28 C.F.R. § 571.60-.64.

For those defendants who were sentenced for offenses that occurred prior to November 1, 1987, the BOP's compassionate release program is governed by 18 U.S.C. § 4205(g). Although that statute was repealed on November 1,

1987, it still applies to inmates whose offenses occurred prior to that date. The repealed law states that under 18 U.S.C. § 4205(g), a sentencing court, on motion of the BOP, may make an inmate with a minimum term sentence immediately eligible for parole by reducing the minimum term of the sentence to time served.

28 C.F.R. § 571.60-.64 (Subpart G)

Title 28 of the Code of Federal Regulations, § 571.60-.64, subpart G, establishes the regulations and process for inmates and BOP staff to initiate and process a request. The C.F.R. reiterates that a request for compassionate release may be initiated only in the event of "extraordinary and compelling" circumstances, but does not provide any more definition than the U.S. Code as to what circumstances might apply.

U.S. Sentencing Commission Guidelines

The U.S. Sentencing Commission (USSC) is an independent federal agency within the judicial branch that develops sentencing policies and guidelines for use by judges in the federal courts. Pursuant to a congressional directive, the USSC developed a policy statement to clarify what constitutes "extraordinary and compelling" circumstances under 18 U.S.C. § 3582(c)(1)(A).[16] The USSC's policy statement provides four examples of circumstances that would constitute "extraordinary and compelling reasons," provided that the defendant is not a danger to the safety of any other person or to the community. According to the USSC guidelines, extraordinary and compelling reasons exist when:

1) The defendant is suffering from a terminal illness.
2) The defendant is suffering from a permanent physical or medical condition, or is experiencing deteriorating physical or mental health because of the aging process, that substantially diminishes the ability of the defendant to provide self-care and for which conventional treatment promises no substantial improvement.
3) The death or incapacitation of the defendant's only family member capable of caring for the defendant's minor child or minor children.
4) Any other circumstance which the Director of the Bureau of Prisons finds to be an extraordinary and compelling reason.[17]

Department Policy

BOP Director Memorandum

On July 22, 1994, the BOP Director issued a memorandum to BOP executive staff regarding compassionate release requests. The memorandum indicated that the BOP had recently expanded its "general guideline" in compassionate release cases to allow inmates with life expectancies of no more than 1 year to be eligible for consideration. According to the memorandum, prior to this revision, the BOP's "general guideline" required that an inmate have a life expectancy of no more than 6 months to be eligible for compassionate release. The memorandum further indicated that, contrary to prior BOP practice, inmates with extremely serious or debilitating medical conditions also were eligible to be considered for compassionate release. The memorandum outlined certain factors for BOP staff to consider in evaluating a request for release, including the nature and circumstances of the inmate's offense, the age of the inmate, and the danger the inmate may pose to the public if released.

BOP Program Statement 5050.46

The BOP's Program Statement, "Compassionate Release, Procedures for Implementation of 18 U.S.C. § 3582(c)(1)(A) and § 4205(g)," was last revised by the BOP on May 19, 1998. It establishes policies and procedures for submitting and reviewing compassionate release requests, and includes processes for considering both medical and non-medical requests. The Program Statement outlines the objectives of the program, including that:

- a motion for a modification of a sentence will be made to the sentencing court only in particularly extraordinary or compelling circumstances that could not reasonably have been foreseen by the court at the time of sentencing,
- the public will be protected from undue risk by careful review of each compassionate release request, and
- compassionate release motions will be filed with the sentencing judge in accordance with the statutory requirements of 18 U.S.C. § 3582(c)(1)(A).

The Program Statement also includes procedures for initiating a request, approval of a request, and denial of a request. In addition, it describes which offenders are ineligible for compassionate release. The procedures contained in the Program Statement are the same as those established in 28 C.F.R. § 571.61-.64.

PURPOSE, SCOPE, AND METHODOLOGY OF THE OIG REVIEW

Purpose

Our review examined the BOP's implementation of its authority to seek from a federal judge a reduction in sentence for inmates for "extraordinary and compelling" reasons and the BOP's process for approving or denying inmate requests pursuant to this authority. Specifically, we examined:

- the BOP's explanation of the program to inmates;
- the policies and procedures to grant compassionate release, including guidance or criteria used to approve or deny requests based on "extraordinary and compelling" circumstances;
- the timeliness of processing requests;
- the costs associated with the custody of compassionate release inmates; and
- the recidivism rates of those inmates approved and released.

Scope and Methodology

Our review encompassed the BOP's process and handling of requests for compassionate release from calendar years 2006 through 2011. While our review focused on the BOP's process, we also reviewed the roles of the USAOs and ODAG in the compassionate release review process. Our review focused on federal offenders, and therefore we did not address state prisoners in BOP custody, military offenders, or D.C. Code offenders.[18]

Our fieldwork, conducted from March 2012 through September 2012, included interviews, data collection and analyses, and document reviews. We interviewed BOP Regional Directors and Central Office staff and officials, and ODAG officials. We also interviewed BOP institution staff and staff at USAOs, and collected information from 100 Wardens through a questionnaire. A detailed description of the methodology of our review is in Appendix II.

RESULTS OF THE REVIEW

The BOP does not properly manage the compassionate release program, resulting in inmates who may be eligible candidates for release not being considered. Problems with the program's management are concentrated in four areas.

- First, the BOP has failed to provide adequate guidance to staff regarding the medical and nonmedical criteria for compassionate release consideration.
- Second, the BOP has no timeliness standards for reviewing compassionate release requests, and timeliness standards for inmate appeals do not consider the special circumstances of medical compassionate release requests.
- Third, the BOP does not have formal procedures to inform inmates about the compassionate release program.
- Fourth, the BOP does not have a system to track compassionate release requests, the timeliness of the review process, or whether decisions made by institution and Regional Office staff are consistent with each other or with BOP policy.

As a result of these multiple failures, we concluded that the implementation of the program is inconsistent and results in ad hoc decision making by the BOP in response to inmate requests. We further found that approximately 13 percent (28 of 208) of the inmates whose release requests had been approved by a Warden and Regional Director died before their requests were decided by the BOP Director. We also found that the compassionate release program could both provide cost savings to the BOP and help it in managing the growing federal prison population. In considering the impact of the program on public safety, we found that a small percentage of inmates were rearrested within 3 years of their release under the compassionate release program.

The BOP Has Not Established Adequate Medical or Non-Medical Guidance for Compassionate Release Consideration

Based on our interviews of BOP institution staff and Central Office officials, our review of case files for all compassionate release requests received by the BOP's Central Office from 2006 through 2011, and our analysis of Warden responses to our questionnaire, we found that the BOP failed to provide institution staff with adequate guidance regarding what an appropriate request for compassionate release is. Neither the BOP's regulations nor its Program Statement define what an "extraordinary and compelling" circumstance is, and neither establishes any criteria for evaluating medical or non-medical requests. We found that this lack of adequate guidance resulted in BOP staff interpreting the Program Statement differently.

Of the 20 institution staff we interviewed, 11 (55 percent) said there was no guidance other than the Program Statement, 5 (25 percent) referred to their institution's supplement to the Program Statement as providing additional guidance, 2 (10 percent) referred to the BOP's publication entitled "Clinical Guidelines: Compassionate Release" (Clinical Guidelines) as providing additional guidance, 1 staff member (5 percent) referred to both the Program Statement and the institution's supplement to the Program Statement as providing guidance, and a doctor (5 percent) from one institution referred to medical data on survival rates of individuals with specific types of cancer as guidance in evaluating inmate requests for compassionate release.

Additionally, although the BOP regulations and Program Statement provide no standards for evaluating a medical request for compassionate release, a 1994 BOP Director memorandum (Memorandum) to BOP executive staff established a 1-year life expectancy as "a general guideline, not a requirement," when considering medical requests for compassionate release (see Appendix III). The Memorandum stated there may be other "extremely serious and debilitating" cases that "fall within the medical arena, but may not be terminal or lend themselves to a precise prediction of life expectancy." The Memorandum further established factors to consider for possible recommendation for release, including: the nature and circumstances of the offense, the age of the inmate, and the danger the inmate may pose to the public if released. The Memorandum specified that these factors were not criteria, but guidelines to be evaluated. Staff was directed to rely on their correctional judgment in making recommendations for compassionate release consideration. However, the Memorandum provided no guidelines to BOP staff for considering non-medical requests.

We found that knowledge of the Memorandum and its use when considering requests was limited. Only the BOP Director and General Counsel referred to the Memorandum when asked if guidance other than the Program Statement is utilized when considering compassionate release requests. The BOP Director said the Memorandum provided "clarity." The General Counsel said there was no guidance other than the Program Statement, but said the Memorandum included "things to look for" when considering compassionate release requests. No other Central Office officials or institution staff who review compassionate release requests referenced the Memorandum as guidance that was being used to consider compassionate release requests.

In the sections below, we discuss our analysis of the BOP Program Statement and the guidance provided by the Program Statement supplements created by BOP institutions, and the BOP Clinical Guidelines. We also discuss Sentencing Guidelines developed by the U.S. Sentencing Commission regarding "extraordinary and compelling" circumstances, as well as the BOP's efforts to revise its regulations and the ODAG's role in reviewing requests for compassionate release.

Neither BOP Regulations Nor the Program Statement Defines What An "Extraordinary and Compelling" Circumstance Is

The BOP regulations and Program Statement provide no criteria for BOP staff to consider in determining whether an "extraordinary and compelling" circumstance exists. The regulations and Program Statement provide no definitions, and neither provides any examples of circumstances that qualify as "extraordinary and compelling." As a result, the BOP staff we interviewed provided us with differing views about the meaning of "extraordinary and compelling."

We found that BOP Central Office staff considered "extraordinary and compelling" circumstances to be either terminally ill medical conditions with a life expectancy of 1 year or less or those who are incapacitated and unable to perform their daily activities – criteria that are found nowhere in the relevant statute, the BOP's regulations, or the BOP's Program Statement. Other Central Office staff said that the BOP also would consider non-medical requests if the inmate was the sole surviving parent or caretaker of a minor child, as provided for in the USSC Sentencing Guidelines (see pages 21 to 22 for more information on the USSC Sentencing Guidelines).

However, staff members at the three institutions where we conducted interviews provided us with varied understandings of those "extraordinary and compelling" circumstances that warrant consideration for compassionate release. For example, a Medical Officer at one institution said, "You can go anywhere with extraordinary and compelling." The Warden at a medical institution told us that determining what is an "extraordinary and compelling" circumstance is a "judgment call" and that he was not sure if there was an existing BOP policy that explained it. An Associate Warden at another medical institution said that he did not know what would constitute "extraordinary and compelling" circumstances.

A Senior Counsel to the Deputy Attorney General, who reviews non-terminal medical cases and non-medical cases for the ODAG, told us that requests are reviewed according to the statute, the BOP's regulations, and the BOP's Program Statement.[19] However, as we discuss above, these provide no criteria, definitions, or examples of circumstances that qualify as "extraordinary and compelling." The Senior Counsel also told us that when reviewing requests she weighs factors consistent with those considered by the BOP to determine whether a particular case involves extraordinary and compelling circumstances that warrant submission of a compassionate release motion to a sentencing judge. For each medical request, the BOP provides memoranda to ODAG which describe whether the inmate is severely debilitated, among other information relating to a number of factors including any proposed release plan and any public safety risk posed by the inmate's release.

Institution Program Statement Supplements

BOP policy permits Wardens to issue supplements for their institutions in implementing BOP directives, including Program Statements, program manuals, and operational manuals. An institution supplement may not detract from or replace the BOP directive it implements. The BOP's Deputy General Counsel said that national policy is "a broad brush approach" and that institution supplements have more specific steps for the institution. We found that the BOP's Central Office does not approve or review institution supplements. Rather, each Warden appoints a Directives Manager who ensures that institution supplements are in compliance with national policy.

All three institutions where we conducted interviews had supplements to the BOP's compassionate release Program Statement. We reviewed these supplements and found that they were inconsistent with one another in providing guidance on what circumstances were "extraordinary and compelling." For example, one of the three institution supplements defined compassionate release as "release from incarceration because of a terminal illness with a life expectancy of less than one year, or when extraordinary or compelling circumstances warrant release." The second institution's supplement defined compassionate release as ". . . release due to extraordinary circumstances or compelling circumstances which could not reasonably have been foreseen by the court at the time of sentencing (i.e., terminal illness)."[20] The supplement for the third institution stated that "when inmates are suitable candidates for reduction in sentence (compassionate release) due to a medical reason and appropriate arrangements can be made, the institution should expedite processing of the release action." None of the three institution supplements provided guidance on what debilitating medical conditions or non-medical requests would be eligible for consideration under the program.[21]

The BOP Program Statement Does Not Adequately Describe What Medical Conditions Are Appropriate for Compassionate Release Consideration

The Program Statement establishes a process for reviewing medical requests, but does not provide any guidance on what medical conditions are appropriate for consideration.[22] For example, the BOP's Medical Director, who is responsible for providing recommendations to the BOP Director for requests that already have been approved by a Warden and Regional Director, said he believes terminally ill inmates include those with a life expectancy of 6 to 12 months. The Medical Director further stated that predicting life expectancy is not an exact science and that there is no hard data that accurately predicts life expectancy.[23] Life expectancy is not specified in the BOP's Program Statement and is not even cited as a factor that the BOP considers. The BOP's Medical Director also said there has been an increased focus on incapacitated inmates, including those with debilitating medical conditions. Again, there are no medical criteria in the BOP's Program Statement regarding inmates that are medically incapacitated. The Medical Director added that when he reviews requests from inmates who are medically incapacitated he considers the inmates' ability to conduct their own daily living activities, as well as the inmates' mental status. Neither of these factors is mentioned in the Program Statement.

Given that the opinion of the BOP Medical Director is solicited only after an inmate's request has been recommended for approval by the Warden and the Regional Director, Wardens and Regional Directors are deciding inmate requests for compassionate release without the benefit of any guidance from the Medical Director. Furthermore, if a medical request is denied by the Warden or Regional Director for reasons that are inconsistent with the Medical Director's views, absent an inmate appeal, the Medical Director will likely never be made aware of the inmate's request because the request is not sent to the BOP's Central Office and the decisions of Wardens and Regional Directors are not subjected to any systematic reviews.

Based on our interviews with Central Office officials and staff, as well as our review of "talking points" prepared for presentations by the BOP's

General Counsel to Wardens and other BOP staff (see Appendix IV), we found that the medical criteria that BOP Central Office officials and staff applied when considering compassionate release requests were whether:

- inmates had a "[t]erminal illness," which was defined as having a life expectancy of 1 year or less, or
- inmates were "[s]everely physically or cognitively debilitated which significantly impairs physical and/or mental function and will not improve with treatment seriously limits daily activities."

The BOP also provided the OIG with two sets of training materials prepared by the BOP Office of General Counsel – one for legal staff and one for medical staff, social workers, and new Wardens in Federal Medical Centers. The training materials for legal staff included the medical criteria described above. The training materials for medical staff, social workers, and new Wardens in Federal Medical Centers included the medical criteria described above, as well as specific examples of medical conditions and factors establishing debilitating conditions. However, based on our interviews with staff at three institutions, we concluded that these training materials were not provided to all institution staff that review inmate requests.

Furthermore, not all of the staff members we interviewed at the three institutions were aware of the medical criteria described above. At one medical institution, we were provided with three different criteria for evaluating medical requests. Specifically, the chief of a group of staff doctors at that medical institution who reviewed compassionate release requests from inmates with cancer said he approves requests only where the inmate has a life expectancy of 6 months or less. He added that if the medical group at the institution does not approve a request, the request does not move forward to the institution's multi-disciplinary committee for a vote on the request.[24] By contrast, the chair of the institution's committee said that to receive approval for compassionate release an inmate's life expectancy must be 1 year or less, but also indicated that this criterion is not written in policy. The Associate Warden at the institution had yet another view, telling us that "terminally ill" is not an officially defined term at the institution.

Similarly, at another medical institution where we conducted interviews, the Director of Nursing, who is a voting member of the institution's committee that determines whether to approve compassionate release requests, explained that the "threshold" necessary for approval of a medical request is a life expectancy of 6 months or less. By contrast, a Unit Manager at the same medical institution, who also is a voting member of the institution's review committee, said there was no specific definition of "terminally ill."

Finally, we were told by a Case Management Coordinator at a nonmedical institution, who reviews requests for compliance with BOP policy, that the BOP does not define terminal illness. As noted above, that is indeed what we found in our review of the BOP's regulations and Program Statement.

Clinical Guidelines

As stated earlier, two institution staff we interviewed said they refer to the BOP's Clinical Guidelines to determine whether an inmate who requests compassionate release is eligible for consideration. We found that these Clinical Guidelines include definitions of terminal illness, life expectancy, and compassionate release; program objectives; and other factors to be considered by staff involved in the assessment of a request. For example, the Clinical Guidelines define life expectancy as "a clinical attempt to quantify the time that a terminally ill patient has remaining. This estimate is made by the attending physician, and is based on the progression of the illness as determined through collective medical experience and literature." Other factors to be considered include: (1) the nature and circumstances of the offense; (2) the criminal and personal history, and characteristics of the inmate; (3) the likelihood that the inmate will participate in criminal activities if released; (4) the inmate's current age and his or her age at the time of sentencing; (5) the danger, if any, the inmate poses to the public or himself or herself if released; (6) the length of sentence imposed and the amount of time left to serve on the sentence; (7) appropriateness of the release plan; and (8) whether the inmate's condition can be remedied by an organ transplant.

The Clinical Guidelines also contain medical criteria for "an appropriate request [that] would encompass extraordinary and compelling circumstances entailing the inmate's medical conditioning which the court was not aware of or foreseen during the time of sentencing." The medical criteria include:

- a terminal illness, with a life expectancy of 1 year or less;
- a progressive debilitating medical condition that seriously limits an individual's daily activities and that cannot be stabilized by either medication or other medical procedures;
- a severe, permanent cognitive condition that significantly impairs physical or mental function and will not improve with treatment; and
- advanced physically limiting factors.

However, the Clinical Guidelines do not provide any examples of debilitating medical conditions, such as those provided in the training material discussed above, and do not address non-medical requests for compassionate release. In addition, only 2 of 20 (10 percent) institution staff we interviewed referred to the Clinical Guidelines as "guidance" for reviewing compassionate release requests. Also, when we asked Wardens in our questionnaire to describe the available resources for considering medical requests for compassionate release, only 3 of the 100 (3 percent) who responded referenced the BOP's Clinical Guidelines.[25] Furthermore, when we requested the Clinical Guidelines from the BOP's Central Office, we were told that the BOP does not have Clinical Guidelines for compassionate release. Subsequently, we requested and received the Clincial Guidelines from the institution staff who had told us that they used the Clinical Guidelines to review compassionate release requests.

Given the response from the BOP's Central Office that the Clinical Guidelines did not exist, even though they did, and the limited number of staff that told us they used the Guidelines as a resource, we concluded that the Clinical Guidelines likely are not used by the vast majority of BOP institution staff when considering compassionate release requests for medical reasons and that institution staff are generally unaware of them.

The BOP's Program Statement Does Not Establish What Non-Medical Circumstances Are Appropriate for Compassionate Release Consideration

Although the BOP's regulations and Program Statement do not limit compassionate release requests to medical requests, the BOP has stated that it routinely denies non-medical requests. As described below, our review confirmed that the BOP did not approve, from 2006 to 2011, any non-medical requests for compassionate release despite its legal authority to do so.

In December 2006, the BOP sought to formalize this practice by amending its regulations. It published a proposed rule that would have changed the title of its compassionate release regulation from "Compassionate Release" to "Reduction in Sentence for Medical Reasons" and restricted its authority under 18 U.S.C. §§ 3582(c)(1)(A)(i) and 4205(g) to two classes of medical cases: (1) where a prisoner is terminally ill with a life expectancy of less than a year and (2) where a prisoner has a "profoundly debilitating medical condition" that "eliminates or severely limits the inmate's ability to attend to fundamental bodily functions and personal care needs." Thus, under the proposed rule, a non-medical condition no longer would qualify as an "extraordinary and compelling" reason for seeking a reduction in sentence. At the time, the BOP explained that the purpose of the proposed revision was to "more accurately reflect our authority under these statutes and our current policy." The BOP further stated in its proposed rulemaking that the BOP "has received letters and Administrative Remedy appeals from inmates who mistakenly believe that we will consider circumstances other than the inmate's medical condition for reducing a sentence. Such is not the Bureau's practice. We believe this title more accurately describes our criteria and procedures." Although the comment period for the proposed revised regulation ended in February 2007, it appears that the rule remains pending without any action having been taken on it by the BOP or the Department.

Consistent with the BOP's statement in 2006, we were told by BOP staff, and our review of BOP training materials confirmed, that the BOP's practice was to reject non-medical requests for compassionate release, despite the fact that Congress did not limit "extraordinary and compelling" circumstances to only medical conditions and that both the BOP's current regulations and its Program Statement provide for consideration of nonmedical compassionate release requests. We found that the BOP did not approve a single non-medical compassionate release request from 2006 through 2011, although two non-medical requests were forwarded to the BOP's Central Office and denied by the BOP Director.

We were unable to determine how many non-medical requests were made during this period by inmates but rejected prior to reaching the BOP Director because, as discussed below, BOP records were not maintained in a manner that enabled such a review. However, institution staff we interviewed reported receiving non-medical requests from inmates, and they provided us with examples of the circumstances involved. For example, the Chief Social Worker at one institution said the institution received one to two non-medical requests each year. She said that a request may involve an inmate who had a child with a medical condition and who wanted to be able to care for the child. The Health Services Administrator at the same institution explained that a non-medical request may include an inmate whose family member was caring for the inmate's child but the family member was unable to continue caring for the child and the inmate was the only other person available, or an inmate who had diminished mental status and did not even know he or she was being punished and was not at risk of re-offending.

USSC Sentencing Guidelines

When we asked the BOP's General Counsel under what circumstances the BOP would consider a non-medical request, she cited the circumstances listed in the USSC Sentencing Guidelines. The BOP Director also told us that BOP staff should be using the USSC Sentencing Guidelines when considering a request. However, institution staff we interviewed were either unaware of the Sentencing Guidelines or did not know that they are authorized to consider inmate requests that were consistent with the Sentencing Guidelines. For example, we spoke with an Associate Warden at a medical institution, who was also a voting member of the institution's committee that determines if an inmate request is appropriate for compassionate release. While the Associate Warden was aware of the Sentencing Guidelines, the Associate Warden did not follow them in considering requests and instead followed the BOP's Program Statement.

We reviewed the regulations and Program Statement and found they do not mention the Sentencing Guidelines. We also reviewed the General Counsel's "talking points" for presentations to Wardens and other BOP staff as well as training materials provided by the BOP, both of which are discussed above, and found that each referenced the Sentencing Guidelines. However, we believe that the references to the Sentencing Guidelines in these materials were confusing and did not clearly state whether BOP personnel were authorized to consider the circumstances established in the Sentencing Guidelines when evaluating inmate compassionate release requests, particularly in non-medical circumstances.

For example, the "talking points" state, "Do not summarily deny cases that fall within these [sentencing] guideline parameters but outside BOP criteria. Denials of these requests should address these issues but stay within BOP medical criteria." In addition, training materials for legal staff stated that the examples cited in the Sentencing Guidelines "are broader than criteria historically used by the BOP in deciding whether to make such motions" and that the BOP's practice was to consider only the medical condition of the inmate. Similarly, the training materials for medical staff, social workers, and new Wardens in Federal Medical Centers included the Sentencing Guidelines as "non-medical issues to ponder," but under the heading "extraordinary and compelling" stated that "the BOP has always narrowly interpreted the statute" and listed the following as extraordinary and compelling circumstances:

- Condition not reasonably foreseen at sentencing, [and]
- Medical condition terminal within one year, or

- Medical condition with indeterminate life expectancy but,
  - severely debilitating [and] irreversible cognitive or physical medical condition,
  - limited or unable to attend to ADLs (activities of daily living).

While these training materials were created for medical staff, social workers, and new Wardens in Federal Medical Centers, none of the three Wardens at the institutions where we conducted interviews, including two medical institutions, were aware of the possible relationship between considering "extraordinary and compelling" circumstances and the Sentencing Guidelines. Additionally, a social worker we interviewed who chairs the institution's multi-disciplinary committee that votes to approve or deny compassionate release requests said she was not that familiar with the relevant policy statement in the Sentencing Guidelines.

As stated earlier, we found only two non-medical inmate requests that were received and reviewed by the BOP Director from 2006 through 2011. In each case, the inmate cited the Sentencing Guidelines as the basis for the request. In the first case, an inmate requested compassionate release because the family caregiver of the inmate's minor children had died of cancer. The inmate's request was denied by the BOP Director because of concerns about whether the inmate would be "able to sustain the stresses of sole parenting and employment while remaining crime-free." In the second case, the inmate requested compassionate release because of his wife's deteriorating health and the medical condition of one of his adult daughters. The inmate's request was denied by the BOP Director because the BOP Director found that the judge was aware at the time of sentencing of the medical conditions of the inmate's wife and daughter, that other family members were available to assist with the care of the wife and daughter, and that the inmate would be eligible for home confinement in 9 months from the date of denial of the request.

ODAG Review of Compassionate Release Requests

The regulations and Program Statement establish the roles for BOP and USAO officials when reviewing compassionate release requests. However, we found that the ODAG reviews non-medical requests for compassionate release as well as medical requests from inmates who are severely and permanently mentally or physically debilitated but whose life expectancy is indeterminate or unknown (non-terminal).

The BOP's General Counsel explained that the ODAG review of compassionate release requests stems from a verbal agreement between the

BOP and ODAG that originated during the Department's consideration of the BOP's 2006 draft regulations (discussed above and below). During our case file review, we found a document entitled, "ODAG Notification Requirement in BOP Policy." The document states that the BOP is required to notify the ODAG of all non-terminal compassionate release requests that have been approved by the BOP Director: "Once approved by the Director . . . materials must be immediately forwarded to the ODAG . . . Further processing in non-terminal cases will occur two business days after submission to the ODAG, absent objections or concerns raised by that office to the Director . . . ." The document also requires the BOP to provide a quarterly report to the ODAG on all non-terminal compassionate release requests that were approved.

The document further states that the requirement that the BOP notify the ODAG "will be in policy and not in the federal regulation as it is a high-level, purely internal, execute [sic] branch operating procedure." The document further states that placing the ODAG notification "in the regulations could unnecessarily subject ODAG to judicial requests, congressional inquiries/demands, and civil liability." When we attempted to determine the origin of the document and the processes that it implemented, we found that no BOP or ODAG official was aware of the document, including how it originated or who wrote it and approved the requirements established in the document.

Based on our case file review, we found that 26 requests for compassionate release since 2006 that were forwarded to the BOP's Central Office for consideration by the BOP Director fell into the two categories requiring ODAG review, with 24 involving non-terminal medical requests and 2 involving non-medical requests. For the 24 non-terminal medical requests, 15 case files contained documentation, such as an e-mail from ODAG staff or handwritten notes from BOP staff verifying that the ODAG reviewed the request and had "approved," or did "not oppose," the BOP's recommendation to approve a request. We found no information in the remaining nine case files to indicate whether the ODAG had reviewed the requests, which were ultimately approved by the BOP Director. For the two non-medical requests forwarded to the BOP Central office, we found documentation in one of them that the case was forwarded to the ODAG for review, but we did not find a response. The other file had no information as to whether the ODAG had reviewed the request, and we found that the BOP Director had denied the request.[26]

Denial of Compassionate Release for Inmate in Vegetative State

In 2006, the BOP received a medical request for compassionate release on behalf of an inmate who had suffered a "massive stroke." The inmate was in a near vegetative state but his medical condition was not considered terminal. BOP records state that staff fed and provided medication to the inmate through a feeding tube, turned and repositioned the inmate every 2 hours, administered toileting, and bathed the inmate two to three times a week and as needed.

The inmate was serving a life sentence for distributing cocaine and conspiring to distribute cocaine and heroin. The inmate had prior convictions for theft and failure to appear, possession with intent to distribute cocaine, and common law assault.

The BOP Director recommended approval of the request "due to [the inmate's] totally debilitated medical condition and near-vegetative condition with no hope of recovery." Because the inmate's life expectancy was indeterminate, the request was referred to the ODAG for review. The ODAG subsequently responded, "Please be advised that ODAG does not concur with the proposed release of [the inmate] at this time." The inmate is still incarcerated at a BOP medical institution and, according to the BOP, while he is no longer in a near-vegetative state, the right side of his body remains paralyzed (the medical center's clinical director has concluded that the inmate has no hope of recovering any function to the right side of his body), he cannot speak, and he needs total assistance with his activities of daily living.

Source: BOP.

A Senior Counsel to the Deputy Attorney General said that since she began reviewing requests in 2011, the ODAG has not objected to any BOP recommendations. However, the Senior Counsel also said that there is no protocol for those circumstances where there is a disagreement between the ODAG and the BOP. The BOP's General Counsel said there has been only one disagreement between the ODAG and the BOP and that case involved a request in 2006 on behalf of an inmate who had suffered a stroke and was in a vegetative state. We reviewed the case file for this inmate and found that the BOP Director had approved the request, that the ODAG had opposed the request, and that the request was ultimately denied (see textbox).

Efforts by the BOP to Revise Its Regulations Governing Compassionate Release Have Been Unsuccessful

The BOP's Program Statement, which contains the same procedures for reviewing compassionate release requests as those established in the regulations, was last revised in 1998. As noted above, on December 21, 2006, the BOP published proposed revisions to its regulations regarding compassionate release. The proposed revisions would have excluded non-medical conditions from being considered as a basis for compassionate release and would have limited medical conditions that were an appropriate basis for compassionate relief to situations where:

- the inmate suffers from a terminal illness with a life expectancy of 1 year or less, or
- the inmate has a profoundly debilitating medical condition that may be physical or cognitive in nature, is irreversible and cannot be remedied through medication or other measures, and has eliminated or severely limited the inmate's ability to attend to fundamental bodily functions and personal care needs without substantial assistance from others (including personal hygiene and toilet functions, basic nutrition, medical care, and maintaining physical safety).

Following the public comment period, however, the Department never issued final regulations and the proposed regulations remain pending. A current Senior Counsel in the ODAG who reviews both non-terminal and non-medical compassionate release requests told us that the 2006 proposed rule was developed through a process involving the ODAG, BOP, Criminal Division, and Office of Legal Policy (OLP). In 2008, the BOP sent a proposed final rule to OLP that differed significantly from the proposed rule published in 2006. The BOP's proposed final rule broadened, rather than restricted, the circumstances for seeking reductions in sentences. We were told that OLP had various concerns about the BOP's proposed final rule, including:

1) while the 2006 proposed rule limited BOP consideration of compassionate release requests to those based on medical circumstances, the 2008 proposed final rule would have permitted the BOP to seek reductions of sentence on both medical and nonmedical grounds;
2) the 2008 proposed final rule's description of medical criteria for a compassionate release request based on non-terminal medical

circumstances would have allowed reductions in sentences more broadly than the profound debilitation standard reflected in the 2006 proposed rule; and

3) the 2008 proposed final rule no longer required USAO concurrence with the BOP General Counsel's decision to pursue a compassionate release case and refer the case to the Director.

In light of OLP's concerns, the BOP advised OLP in 2011 that it had decided not to pursue these revisions. A BOP Assistant General Counsel stated that the Department in 2008 did not like the BOP's proposed revisions because it thought the BOP was dramatically expanding its criteria for compassionate release, even though the BOP believed it was simply clarifying its medical criteria. We also were told by the BOP's Deputy General Counsel that in 2008 the Department expressed concerns about a perceived expansion of the medical conditions that might result in a dramatic increase in the number of inmate requests and releases pursuant to the statutory authority.

The BOP's General Counsel told us that the BOP is currently attempting to revise its compassionate release regulations once again. The General Counsel also said that after the new regulations are adopted, the BOP would revise the Program Statement, a process that would take about 2 years once new regulations are in place due to the requirement that the BOP negotiate changes to the Program Statement with its union.[27] Several officials from the BOP Central Office and the ODAG told us that the BOP is separately drafting a new guidance memorandum for medical institutions that will expand the compassionate release program by making inmates with a life expectancy of up to 18 months eligible for consideration. The new memorandum is also intended to assist staff who review compassionate release requests in understanding what level of functioning is sufficiently "extraordinary and compelling" for inmates with debilitating medical conditions to be considered for release. The BOP did not provide the OIG with a copy of the memorandum under consideration and could not tell us when it would be finalized.

We believe that revised regulations, and subsequently a revised Program Statement, would benefit the BOP's management of its compassionate release program. Specifically, regulations and a Program Statement that accurately reflect the BOP's criteria for determining eligible medical and non-medical requests would provide all BOP staff clear and comprehensive standards for understanding what "extraordinary and compelling" circumstances warrant consideration for compassionate release. In addition, while the BOP did not provide the OIG with a copy of this new guidance under consideration, and did not know when the changes would be finalized, we believe that the new guidance described to us would result in cost savings for the BOP, as well as alleviate its population management difficulties by enabling more inmates to be eligible for compassionate release consideration. We discuss potential cost savings and population management in more detail later in the report.

Conclusion

The BOP does not provide the staff of its institutions with adequate guidance regarding what the appropriate basis is for evaluating a compassionate release request. As a consequence, we found that institutions were applying different and inconsistent standards. We further found that not all institution staff knew the circumstances under which a request for compassionate release is appropriate because the BOP's Program Statement, most commonly used by staff to consider a request for compassionate release, does not establish appropriate medical or non-medical circumstances for consideration. In addition, supplements created by institution staff do not adequately describe the circumstances that would warrant favorable consideration for compassionate release. Because BOP staff primarily use an inadequate Program Statement that was last revised in 1998 as their only policy guidance to determine appropriate candidates for the program, we concluded that requests from potentially eligible inmates may not be considered favorably at the institution and regional levels and may never be considered by the BOP Director. The BOP needs to update its regulations and Program Statement to accurately reflect what would make both medical and non-medical requests appropriate for consideration, as well as to include all aspects of the review process, including that of the ODAG.

The BOP has no timeliness standards for reviewing compassionate release requests, and timeliness standards for inmate appeals do not consider the special circumstances of medical compassionate release requests.

The BOP's compassionate release regulations provide that a request for release based on an inmate's medical condition "shall [be] expedite[d] . . . at all levels." The BOP's Program Statement directs institutions to review requests "promptly" and, in the case of medical requests, indicates that staff should "expedite" such requests. The Program Statement, however, does not specify a timeframe for reviewing requests, which we found resulted in BOP staff members interpreting the Program Statement's direction regarding timeliness differently.[28] In addition, the process inmates can use to appeal a Warden's or Regional Director's denial of a compassionate release request can take more than 5 months to complete.

The BOP's Program Statement Does Not Establish Timeliness Standards for Reviewing Requests

The BOP's Program Statement states, "The Warden shall promptly review a request for consideration," and, "in the event the basis of the request is the medical condition of the inmate, staff shall expedite the request at all levels." A BOP Assistant General Counsel told us that institutions are asked to expedite all requests, but case-by-case factors affect timeliness and deadlines are difficult to impose because of the numerous factors involved in evaluating requests. A BOP Senior Counsel stated that there are no timeframes because of the unexpected and individualized nature of each request.

Because the BOP does not provide a timeframe, we found various BOP staff members interpret the Program Statement's direction regarding timeliness differently. For example, a Warden stated that the general expectation at his institution was to process requests in 5 days. An Associate Warden at another institution stated that her institution had expectations to process requests in less than 30 days. In response to our questionnaire, only 33 out of 100 Wardens (33 percent) reported having a designated timeframe for reviewing requests at their institution. For those institutions that reported having a timeframe, the timeframe ranged from 5 to 65 days.

The BOP's Timeliness Standards for Inmate Appeals Do Not Consider the Special Circumstances of Medical Compassionate Release Requests

The BOP's administrative remedy program allows an inmate to seek formal review by higher level BOP officials of an issue relating to any aspect of his or her incarceration. Procedures, including timeliness standards, for an inmate to seek an appeal are established in the administrative remedy Program Statement.[29] However, we found that the procedures and timeliness standards do not reference the compassionate release program or acknowledge the special circumstances of an inmate requesting compassionate release (particularly those with terminal medical conditions and limited life expectancies).

Before an inmate can submit an appeal under the administrative remedy program, the inmate must first discuss the concern informally with institution staff and institution staff must attempt to informally resolve the inmate's concern. Although Wardens must establish procedures for informal resolution of inmate concerns and ensure that informal resolution is made in an orderly and timely manner, the Program Statement for the administrative remedy program does not specify timeliness standards for this informal resolution process.[30]

If informal resolution does not resolve an inmate's concern, an inmate may submit a formal written administrative remedy request to the Warden. Once a request is filed, the Warden must respond within 20 calendar days. An inmate that is not satisfied with the Warden's response may appeal to the appropriate Regional Director. The Regional Director must respond within 30 calendar days. Finally, an inmate not satisfied with the Regional Director's response may appeal to the BOP's General Counsel, which is the final avenue for an administrative appeal. The General Counsel must respond within 40 calendar days of the date of the inmate's appeal.

As a result, an inmate could wait up to 90 days (not including the time for the informal resolution process to be concluded and for the inmate to prepare the submission for each appeal) if the inmate seeks an appeal at all levels of the review process. However, the administrative remedy Program Statement allows officials at all levels of the appeal process to extend their response time if they believe the established timeliness standards do not provide sufficient time to respond. Thus, a Warden's response time may be extended from 20 to 40 days, a Regional Director's response time may be extended from 30 to 60 days, and the General Counsel's response time may be extended from 40 to 60 days. As a result, an inmate could wait up to 160 days (or over 5 months) for completion of the appeal process if the officials at each level of review extended their time to respond.[31] For inmates with terminal medical conditions and life expectancies of less than 1 year, which we found are generally the only inmates whose compassionate release requests are given serious consideration by the BOP, these timeliness standards likely provide little to no meaningful opportunity to pursue an appeal.

We found that, in connection with an appeal of a compassionate release denial, there is little reason for the BOP to mandate an informal resolution process at the institution level or to require that the Warden review an inmate's appeal, given that the Warden has previously either denied the compassionate release request or approved it (in which case denial was by the Regional Director because inmates cannot appeal the BOP Director's final decision). While the administrative remedy Program Statement waives the requirement that the initial appeal be considered at the institution level in four limited circumstances, a compassionate release appeal is not listed as one of those circumstances. Additionally, we found that, in those circumstances where the

Regional Director denied the inmate's request following approval by the Warden, there is little reason to provide the Regional Director with a lengthy period of time to consider the appeal.

Conclusion

The BOP's compassionate release Program Statement does not specify a timeframe for reviewing requests, resulting in BOP staff members interpreting the Program Statement's direction regarding timeliness differently. While the OIG recognizes the complexity and importance of the compassionate release review process, given the time-sensitive nature of these requests, particularly for inmates with terminal medical conditions and limited life expectancies, we concluded that the BOP must establish timeliness standards for each step in the review process. We also concluded that the timeframes established in the administrative remedy Program Statement do not take into account the special circumstances of compassionate release requests, particularly for inmates who are terminally ill and have a life expectancy of less than 1 year. We found that the usual timeframes for handling appeals, including those for denials of inmate requests for compassionate release are at least in some circumstances, unnecessarily lengthy.

The BOP does not have formal procedures to inform inmates about the compassionate release program.

The BOP does not require institution staff to inform inmates about the compassionate release program. Additionally, we found that few BOP institutions include information about the compassionate release program in their institution handbooks.[32] We also found that, in the absence of policy or procedures, methods used to inform inmates about the compassionate release program vary. We concluded that potentially appropriate inmates may not know about the compassionate release program and, as a result, inmates who may be strong candidates for compassionate release never request consideration.

Staff Is Not Required to Inform Inmates About the Program

Neither the federal regulations establishing the compassionate release program nor the BOP's compassionate release Program Statement specify how inmates are to be informed about the program.[33] BOP institutions conduct admission and orientation (A&O) programs for new inmates to provide them with general information regarding institution-wide regulations, operations, and program opportunities.[34] The BOP's A&O Program Statement requires that specific program information be discussed with inmates. We found, however, that the compassionate release program was not one of the programs that is required to be discussed during an A&O program.

Institutions have the discretion to supplement required elements of the A&O program with local procedures and program information. Staff members we interviewed at three institutions generally were not aware of whether the compassionate release program was discussed during their institutions' A&O programs. A Medical Officer at one institution said, "It might be glossed over as it so rarely comes up." We reviewed the agenda of the A&O programs at two of the three institutions and found that the compassionate release program was not included. The third institution did not provide us with an A&O program agenda. Rather, the institution provided us with an A&O handbook. We reviewed this A&O handbook and found that the compassionate release program was briefly mentioned, but only as a program for early inmate release in the event of extraordinary and compelling circumstances that could not have been foreseen by the court at the time of sentencing. It provided no clarification as to what circumstances would be appropriate to make a compassionate release request or how to initiate a request. We discuss institution handbooks further below.

Only a Few BOP Institution Handbooks Contain Information About the Program

While not required to do so, most BOP institutions provide a handbook when an inmate arrives at a designated institution. The purpose of the handbooks is to provide inmates with general information regarding the BOP, its programs, and institution rules and regulations they will encounter while incarcerated. Handbooks are not a specific guide to the detailed policies of the BOP, nor do they include all procedures in effect at each BOP institution.

We found that few institution handbooks included information about the compassionate release program. We reviewed 111 of 117 handbooks used by BOP institutions and found only 8 (7 percent) included information regarding compassionate release.[35] The handbooks that included information about the compassionate release program varied in the amount of information provided. Only two of the eight handbooks discussed "terminal illness," and both of those defined a terminal illness as a life expectancy of 1 year or less. Four of the eight handbooks said that inmates had to explain their "extraordinary and compelling circumstances" in making a request. The remaining two handbooks described compassionate release only as a means to request "an unscheduled review," that is, a review in addition to the scheduled program reviews inmates receive from institution staff who discuss the inmate's progress in recommended programs and recommend new programs.[36]

In response to our questionnaire, 12 of 89 Wardens said that their institutions' handbooks were the most common method for making inmates aware of the compassionate release program.[37] However, only 4 of the handbooks from those 12 institutions contained information on the program.[38]

In the Absence of Policy or Procedures, Methods Used to Inform Inmates About the Program Vary

In our questionnaire, we asked Wardens to rank the most common method used to inform inmates about the compassionate release program from among the following options: (1) institution handbook, (2) institution A&O program, (3) program review, and (4) other. The most common response by the Wardens who replied was "other" (see Table 1).

Table 1. Most Common Method Used to Inform Inmates about the Compassionate Release Program

Method	Percentage
"Other" Method	43
Program Review	24
Institution A&O Program	20
Institution Handbook	13

Source: Analysis of OIG questionnaire responses.

The most common "other" methods identified by the Wardens included inmates reading the BOP Program Statement in institution law libraries; discussions with institution staff if an inmate requests information; word of mouth among the inmates, family members, or attorneys; information posted on institution bulletin boards; and information provided on the BOP's public website. One Warden stated, "As far as I can tell, we do not advertise this and inmates have to find out about it on their own."

Institution staff we interviewed said that methods to inform inmates about the program varied and included receiving information through the medical staff, reading the BOP Program Statement, and inmate word of mouth. For example, one Case Manager said inmates are informed by reading the Program Statement in library services, by hearing about it from other inmates, and by asking the unit team. The Director of Nursing at a medical facility said a physician at the institution usually was the person who informed inmates about the program, but that when inmates approached staff about the program, the inmates' understanding of the program was sometimes wrong. At another medical facility, a Case Manager told us that a doctor or social worker may approach an inmate initially to explain the compassionate release program. However, a doctor at this same medical facility said a social worker would inform the inmate about the program, while a social worker said the medical team would inform the inmate about the program.

Conclusion

The BOP does not have formal or standardized procedures to inform inmates about the compassionate release program. Staff is not required to inform inmates about the program. We found that the methods used to inform inmates about the program are informal and vary by institution. As a result, potentially eligible inmates may not know about the compassionate release program.

The BOP does not have a system to track all compassionate release requests, the timeliness of the review process, or whether decisions made by institution and Regional Office staff are consistent with each other or with BOP policy.

The BOP does not require its institutions to track the number of compassionate release requests. The BOP's Central Office informally tracks only those inmate requests that have been forwarded to the Central Office for review by the BOP Director after they have been approved by both a Warden and a Regional Director. Therefore, the BOP does not know the total number of inmate requests for compassionate release. Also, the BOP does not track the timeliness of institutions or Regional Offices in reviewing requests. As a result, the BOP cannot determine how long the review process takes and where, if any, delays occur in the process. In addition, the BOP cannot determine whether decisions made by institution and Regional Office staff are consistent with each other or with BOP policy.

The BOP Does Not Have A System To Track All Compassionate Release Requests

From 2006 through 2011, the BOP Director considered 211 compassionate release requests that had been approved by a Warden and a Regional Director.[39] Of the 208 requests we reviewed, we found that 206 requests were for medical reasons and 2 requests were for nonmedical reasons. The BOP Director approved 142 (68 percent) of the requests and denied 38 (18 percent). See Appendix V for the reasons the BOP Director approved or denied these requests. In 28 cases (13 percent), the inmates died before a decision was made by the BOP Director.

However, the 211 requests do not represent all compassionate release requests made by inmates during this period. Inmate requests are tracked by the BOP only after a request is approved by both the Warden and the Regional Director, and is received by the BOP's Central Office. Also, we found that institutions do not consistently track inmate requests for compassionate release. As a result, the number of compassionate release requests made by inmates during this period cannot be determined.

Inmate Requests Are Tracked at the BOP's Central Office Only after the Warden and Regional Director Have Approved a Request

We found that the BOP does not know the total number of requests inmates make because the BOP does not track requests denied by Wardens or Regional Directors and does not maintain a centralized system to track all requests. The only requests that the BOP can account for are those that are approved by the Warden and Regional Director and forwarded to the BOP's Central Office for review by the General Counsel and the BOP Director. Requests received by the BOP's Central Office are tracked by the BOP's Office of General Counsel. An Assistant General Counsel told us that there is no way for the Office of General Counsel to capture data at the Warden or Regional Director level because these requests are not tracked at those levels. The BOP's Deputy General Counsel said the only data on the number of denials by Wardens or Regional Directors comes from the BOP's administrative remedy procedure, which reflects only denials that are appealed.

The BOP's compassionate release Program Statement does not require institution or Central Office staff to track compassionate release requests made by inmates. Nevertheless, we found that some institutions do track inmate requests. In our questionnaire to Wardens, we asked whether inmate requests for compassionate release were tracked. Forty-seven of the 98 Wardens who responded (48 percent) said requests were tracked.[40] The Wardens who indicated that their institutions tracked requests stated that it was done through different methods, for example: (1) through a logbook, (2) through a local electronic recording system, or (3) in the inmate's central file.

At two of the three institutions where we conducted interviews the staff members who oversaw compassionate release requests tracked and documented the request process for each inmate and where they were in the review process. The third institution did not have a method in place to track compassionate release requests. In addition, only two of the six Regional Directors' offices tracked inmate requests that they received from institutions. One Regional Director provided the OIG with a spreadsheet indicating the number of compassionate release requests his office received from institutions from 2006 through 2011, as well as the number of requests that were approved by the Regional Director and forwarded to the BOP's Central Office for review. A second Regional Director also provided the OIG with a spreadsheet of requests received from institutions in 2011. However, we found that data tracked by the two Regional Offices varied in consistency and was not complete. For example, while one Regional Office tracked the final disposition of each request, the other Regional Office did not. In addition, dates indicating movement of the request through the review process were not complete.

We were told that while the BOP case management system, SENTRY, has a code specifically for compassionate release, it is not used to account for or track requests but just to identify inmates who are actually released on that basis.[41] We reviewed a report generated from the SENTRY database that the BOP's Office of General Counsel told us identified inmates who had been released through the compassionate release program. The report identified 27 inmates as having been released from BOP custody between 2006 through 2011 under the compassionate release program. However, as stated above, our case file review found that the BOP Director approved 142 inmates during that period for compassionate release. In addition, only 15 of the 27 inmates identified in the SENTRY report were among the 142 inmates that we determined had received compassionate release.[42] Moreover, institution staff members we interviewed were not aware of the SENTRY tracking code or its purpose. The BOP reported that it had not taken any action to direct the use of the SENTRY code for compassionate release, but had alerted staff at the BOP's Designation and Sentence Computation Center to the issue.[43]

The Number of Requests Denied by Wardens and Regional Directors May Be Considerable

Given the absence of a system to track inmate requests for compassionate release, neither the BOP nor the OIG can determine how many inmates submitted requests during the period covered by our review. An Assistant General Counsel told us that the BOP Central Office could determine the total number of requests by asking the institutions how many they received, but the Central Office has never done so. The questionnaire we distributed to Wardens asked them to approximate the number of compassionate release requests that inmates submitted in 2010 and 2011. In addition, we reviewed administrative remedy data to determine how many inmates appealed Warden or Regional Director decisions denying compassionate release requests.[44] Based on this analysis, we found the number of requests that were denied by the Warden or Regional Director, and therefore were never considered by the BOP Director, may be considerable.

Institution Estimates

In an effort to learn the approximate number of requests for compassionate release each institution has processed, the OIG asked Wardens in a questionnaire to estimate the number of requests their institution received in 2010 and 2011. In response, the Wardens reported roughly 618 requests in 2010 and 2011, including 33 requests for non-medical reasons. Our review of compassionate release case files found that only 64 requests were considered by the BOP Director in 2010 and 2011, including 2 nonmedical requests in 2011.[45] While the Wardens' responses to the OIG were rough estimates, the difference between the estimated number of inmate requests reviewed by Wardens and the actual number of requests reviewed by the BOP Director is likely due to many of the requests being rejected by either the Warden or the Regional Director and never considered by the BOP Central Office.

Administrative Remedy

We reviewed the BOP's administrative remedy data to determine how many inmates appealed Warden or Regional Director decisions to deny compassionate release requests.[46] Based on our analysis, from 2006 through 2011, 273 inmates appealed Warden or Regional Director decisions denying a compassionate release request. Since not all inmates appeal a decision by the Warden or Regional Director to deny a request, the number of denied requests would have been higher.

The BOP Does Not Track the Length of Time Taken to Process Requests

The BOP does not track the length of time it takes to approve or deny requests for compassionate release, in part, because the BOP has not established a formal method for initiating the review process. As a result, neither the OIG nor the BOP can assess the timeliness of the review process. We learned that 28 of the 208 (13 percent) inmates whose requests were approved by both a Warden and Regional Director during the period of our review died before the BOP Director made a decision on the request.[47]

In our review of case files, we were unable to determine a consistent point at which the process even began. An Assistant General Counsel said that start dates are hard to define because a case may have been under discussion weeks before anything is written about it. Another Assistant General Counsel stated that the request process is informal and there is no prescribed form to initiate the process. She also stated that the request can come from an inmate, a family member, or BOP staff. Staff at the three institutions where we conducted interviews also told us that there is no formal method at their institutions for initiating the request process and that inmates may make a request verbally or in writing through an "Inmate Request to Staff Member" form and that requests also may come from a family member or a treating physician.[48]

In our review of case files for inmates whose requests had been forwarded to the BOP Director for consideration, we were able to determine an initiation date in only 40 of the 208 cases (19 percent), and those initiation dates were not consistently supported by a written request by the inmate or other documentation. We found initiation dates on Central Office tracking sheets, letters from an inmate's attorney and, in one case, in a letter from the court to an inmate who requested compassionate release directly from the court.[49] Without formal and consistent initiation dates, the OIG was unable to assess the timeliness of the review process for all cases forwarded to the BOP's Central Office from 2006 through 2011. However, of the 40 requests for which we found an initiation date, 29 were approved and averaged 116 days from the initiation date at the institution to the date of the BOP Director's approval. The 11 requests that were denied averaged 109 days.[50]

BOP Central Office and institution staff told us that a number of factors can delay the processing of a compassionate release request, including notifying victims; contacting family members; consulting external medical specialists regarding an inmate's medical condition; removing detainers; finding placement for an inmate if released, such as a nursing home or extended care facility; verifying information in the inmate's release plan through the U.S. Probation Office; gathering additional information from investigative agencies regarding the inmate's offense; or waiting for the opinions of USAOs or the ODAG on the possible release of the inmate. We found documentation in some case files to suggest that these factors may have delayed requests, but we were unable to measure the amount of time attributable to these delays because dates were not consistently noted in all compassionate release case files.

Staff at the three institutions where we conducted interviews were unable to provide us with estimates of the time it took to process a compassionate release request at their institutions. For example, one doctor said he was not sure of a particular timeline for review. Other institution staff members provided guesses on the timeliness of processing a request at their institution, ranging from 2 weeks to "pretty fast."

Moreover, at each level of the process, we found BOP staff had concerns regarding the timeliness of processing a request. For example, a social worker who serves as the review committee chairperson at her institution said once a request leaves the institution with a recommendation of approval it may be as long as 4 months before a final decision is reached. She added that some inmates do not have 4 months left to live and many of them have died waiting for approval by the BOP Director. A Warden at one institution where we conducted interviews said removing a step in the review process, such as the Regional Director's review of a request, may result in shortening the review process by 1 week, which the Warden indicated could be considerable given the nature of compassionate release requests. A Regional Director told us that some inmates who request compassionate release die while still in custody and in some cases that could be due to delays in processing a request or because the inmate's illness progressed faster than anticipated. An Assistant General Counsel said reviewing an inmate's request is a long process and that some inmates "go downhill" very quickly. We also found indications in the case files of concerns regarding delays in the review process. For example, correspondence between two Central Office officials about an inmate who died during consideration said, "Too long. Wonder why so many delays."

Timeliness of the BOP's Responses to Inmate Appeals of Compassionate Release Decisions

As previously discussed, the BOP's administrative remedy program allows an inmate to seek formal review (appeal) by high-level BOP officials of an issue relating to any aspect of his or her incarceration, including any aspect of a compassionate release request. We reviewed BOP administrative remedy data from 2006 through 2011 and found that 273 inmates filed a total of 636 appeals regarding issues related to a request for compassionate release, including 366 appeals to Regional Directors and 270 appeals to the BOP's General Counsel.[51]

Administrative remedy procedures require that a Regional Director respond to an inmate's appeal within 30 calendar days. Based on our review of BOP administrative remedy data, Regional Directors responded in 19 days, on average. Specifically, we found that Regional Directors responded to an inmate's appeal within 30 calendar days in 306 of 366 (84 percent) cases. However, administrative remedy procedures allow Regional Directors to extend their response to an inmate's appeal by 30 days, thereby providing a Regional Director up to 60 days to respond. We found that a Regional Director exceeded this 60-day response time for 24 of 366 (6 percent) appeals, including 7 appeals that took a Regional Director over 100 days to respond. In one case, a Regional Director took 302 calendar days to respond to an inmate's appeal, according to BOP data.

Furthermore, administrative remedy procedures allow an inmate not satisfied with a Regional Director's response to appeal to the BOP's General Counsel. The General Counsel must respond within 40 calendar days of the date of the inmate's appeal. Based on our review of BOP administrative remedy data, we found that the General Counsel provided a response in 40 days, on average. Specifically, we found that the General Counsel responded within 40 calendar days in 164 of 270 (61 percent) appeals. However, the General Counsel may extend the response to an inmate's appeal by 20 days, thereby providing the General Counsel 60 days to respond. We found that the General Counsel exceeded the 60-day response time for 64 of 270 (24 percent) appeals, including 22 appeals that took the General Counsel over 100 days to respond. In one case, the General Counsel took 303 calendar days to respond to an inmate's appeal, according to BOP data.

The BOP Cannot Determine Whether Decisions Made by Institution znd Regional Office Staff Are Consistent with Each Other or with BOP Policy

The BOP does not review whether decisions made by Wardens or Regional Directors regarding compassionate release requests are consistent with each other or with the BOP's Program Statement and the underlying statutory authority. While the BOP Director must give the final approval for a compassionate release request, the regulations provide that the BOP Director reviews a request only after it has been approved by the Warden and a Regional Director. Thus, if the request is denied by the Warden of the inmate's institution or a Regional Director, the request and the denials are never reviewed by anyone at the BOP's headquarters. The BOP Central Office staff told us that the Central Office became aware of compassionate release denials made by a Warden or Regional Director only when the inmate appealed the denial through the BOP's administrative remedy procedure.

All BOP Central Office staff we interviewed confirmed that there is no mechanism in place to review denials by Wardens or Regional Directors of inmate compassionate release requests to ensure they are consistent with each other and with BOP policy. Although the BOP's Central Office conducts program compliance reviews of the institutions' correctional programs, these reviews do not assess the compassionate release program. The reviews seek to, among other things, ensure that institution staff evaluates the programming needs of inmates and manages the inmates' program participation through coordinated communication, documentation, and accessibility. However, the BOP guidelines for conducting institution program compliance reviews do not include the compassionate release program.[52] The BOP Central Office staff said that the BOP relies on training (discussed previously) to ensure that Wardens make appropriate decisions on compassionate release requests.

Conclusion

While we found limited efforts by institutions and regional offices to track inmate requests, as well as a mechanism within the BOP's case management system to identify inmates released through the compassionate release program, the BOP does not have a system in place to track all compassionate release requests from the outset of the review process to its conclusion. As a result, neither the BOP nor the OIG could determine the total number of compassionate release requests made by inmates between 2006 and 2011. In the absence of a system to track all requests, including the disposition of decisions made on requests at the institution and regional level, the BOP cannot effectively manage the compassionate release program.

In addition, the BOP does not track the time it takes to approve or deny requests for compassionate release, has not established a formal method for initiating the review process, and has failed to put in place timeliness standards for any stage of the review process. As a result, neither the OIG nor the BOP can assess the timeliness of the review process. Moreover, we found that inmates have died while awaiting decisions on their requests. We believe that the BOP must formalize the initiation of the review process and record an initiation date for each case. Establishing a formal initiation method will enable the BOP to analyze the timeliness of each step of the review process to identify delays and the reasons for them, and to provide a basis for taking corrective action.

Finally, we found that the BOP cannot evaluate whether the decisions by Wardens or Regional Directors to deny requests are appropriate because the BOP conducts no tracking or oversight of those decisions. The BOP cannot effectively manage the compassionate release program if it cannot ensure decisions made by the Wardens or Regional Directors are appropriate.

Release of inmates through the compassionate release program provides cost savings for the BOP and helps the BOP with its growing prison population and significant capacity issues.

Although BOP officials and institution staff consistently cited cost savings as a benefit of the compassionate release program, the BOP does not track cost savings associated with the release of inmates under the program. As a result, the BOP is unable to support the potential cost savings from expanding the compassionate release program that it reported to Congress in its FY 2013 budget submission. Nevertheless, it is self-evident that the release from BOP custody of an inmate with a serious or terminal medical condition results in cost savings for the BOP.[53] Perhaps even more significantly, the release of such an inmate provides the BOP with an additional bed space which, given the serious population management challenges facing the BOP, is an important non-monetary benefit. We concluded that the BOP could realize additional cost savings, as well as receive assistance in addressing its population management difficulties, from appropriately expanding the use of the compassionate release program. In the sections below, we discuss the limitations of BOP cost data and the potential for documenting cost savings if those limitations are addressed.

The BOP Does Not Track Costs That Could Be or Are Saved through the Program

The BOP does not track marginal daily costs for incarcerated inmates who are receiving medical care, nor does it track costs related to the care and confinement of inmates diagnosed with a terminal illness or inmates with severely debilitating medical conditions. We also found during this review that the BOP does not track cost data for either the treatment of specific medical conditions or the continuing custody of inmates who may be eligible for compassionate release.

The OIG requested the direct medical care costs incurred by the BOP to house an inmate, including the cost of feeding, clothing, and providing medical care for an inmate. The BOP was unable to provide the information because it does not maintain that data and instead provided the OIG with what is referred to as the "daily medical per capita" costs for all inmates.[54]

Because the BOP does not track costs related to the specific care and confinement of inmates diagnosed with terminal illnesses, or inmates with severely debilitating medical conditions, or other circumstances that would warrant consideration for compassionate release, the OIG was unable to calculate costs associated with housing inmates who may be candidates for compassionate release with an acceptable degree of accuracy. In addition, we believe the "daily medical per capita" costs understate the cost of maintaining the inmates that could be potentially considered for this program because the per capita costs include the cost of treating inmates who are receiving basic medical care, such as preventive care, as well as those who are receiving extensive medical treatments.

We also found that the BOP had not analyzed potential cost savings from the release of inmates under the compassionate release program. Under the BOP's management of the program, inmates who have been considered for compassionate release are special circumstance inmates with a terminal illness or severely debilitated condition. The care for these inmates is unique and likely very expensive, and must be identified individually to understand the per inmate cost. The BOP's Medical Director said that determining cost savings resulting from the compassionate release program would require sophisticated analysis and would be difficult to answer accurately. The BOP's General Counsel said there had been no analysis of how much the program has saved through the release of inmates. She added that determining cost savings was difficult because each inmate's circumstances vary.

The BOP Would Accrue Cost Savings if It Expanded the Criteria for Compassionate Release

What data the BOP does track indicates that the costs of incarcerating inmates at its medical centers are higher than at its other institutions, and that these costs are rising. For example, the FY 2011 annual cost for incarcerating an inmate at all levels of incarceration averaged $28,893, while the annual cost for incarcerating an inmate at a BOP medical center was $57,962. In addition, the average costs for the BOP's medical centers increased by 38 percent from FY 2006 to FY 2011.

As previously stated, BOP Central Office officials told the OIG that the BOP is drafting new guidance for medical institutions that would seek to expand the use of the compassionate release program by expressly allowing inmates with a life expectancy of up to 18 months to be considered for release rather than the 12-month limit that many institutions are currently applying informally. The BOP's General Counsel said the new guidance also would assist institution staff in evaluating inmates with debilitating medical conditions so that staff understood what level of functioning is appropriate for compassionate release consideration.

While the BOP did not provide the OIG with a copy of the new guidance under consideration, and did not know when the changes would be finalized, we believe that the new guidance that was described to us would result in cost savings for the BOP by enabling more inmates to be eligible for release. For example, if clarifying and expanding the medical criteria for compassionate release consideration resulted in releasing 100 inmates with serious medical conditions from the medical referral centers each year, the BOP could potentially realize cost savings of at least $5.8 million annually.[55] As previously stated, only 24 inmates are, on average, released each year through the compassionate release program.[56] Cost savings to the BOP can be determined with greater accuracy only if the BOP improves its collection and analysis of costs associated with incarcerating and providing medical care to those inmates appropriate for compassionate release.

The BOP Does Not Have the Data to Support the Potential Savings from Expanding the Compassionate Release Program That It Reported to Congress

The Department's FY 2013 budget request identified $3.2 million in savings to be achieved by expanding the BOP's compassionate release program. Further, the Department's FY 2013 Performance Budget Congressional Submission stated that "by amending current administratively established policies, the BOP could release more inmates in FY 2013" by expanding the BOP's compassionate release program.[57]

In response to the working draft of this report, the BOP stated that the basis for the estimated cost savings of $3.2 million proposed in the FY 2013 President's Budget was a scenario the BOP developed when contemplating expanding the compassionate release program to inmates in medical centers who had served at least 67 percent of their sentences, were convicted of non-violent and non-sex offenses, and had no violence within the past 5 years. The

BOP stated that it estimated that expanding its use of compassionate release in this way could result in $3.2 million in cost savings, based on an average marginal cost for the number of inmates that met those criteria.

We requested the BOP provide us with all documents related to its plan to expand the compassionate release program and the data and documentation supporting its FY 2013 Performance Budget Submission.[58] The BOP was unable to provide any documents related to its plan to expand the compassionate release program. Further, the BOP told the OIG that the criteria used for calculating potential cost savings was the same for all BOP programs and there was not one specifically developed for the compassionate release program. A Central Office official said she was not aware of any efforts to expand the compassionate release program. She added, "The program is the same as it's always been."

Releasing Eligible Inmates through the Compassionate Release Program Assists the BOP with Managing Its Growing Inmate Population and Significant Capacity Issues

We found that the compassionate release program can help the BOP in managing its growing prison population and its significant capacity issues. In FY 2006, there were 192,584 inmates in BOP custody. As of October 2012, the BOP reported 218,936 inmates in its custody, an increase of nearly 14 percent.[59] The Department has identified the BOP's increasingly severe prison capacity issues as a programmatic material weakness in every Performance and Accountability Report it has issued since 2006. Despite having identified prison capacity as a programmatic material weakness for 7 consecutive years, according to the Government Accountability Office, the BOP's prisons have gone from being 36 percent over rated capacity in FY 2006 to being 39 percent over rated capacity in FY 2011. Moreover, the BOP projects a 15-percent increase in its inmate population by 2020.[60]

While the number of inmates who are appropriate for compassionate release is small in comparison to the BOP's overall prison population, we believe that the serious capacity challenges facing the BOP require its leadership to effectively manage each and every one of its programs that can assist in prison population management, particularly in this instance with a program that Congress has expressly authorized. This opinion was shared by officials and institution staff we interviewed who cited population control as a benefit of the compassionate release program. For example, the BOP Director said the release of even one more inmate would be beneficial in managing the BOP's population.

The OIG could not determine how many inmates might have been appropriate candidates for compassionate release because the BOP does not track the total number of inmates who request compassionate release or the conditions of those whose requests were rejected at the institutional and regional levels. However, at a minimum, inmates with a viable release plan who have been diagnosed with a terminal illness or a severely debilitating medical condition and who do not have a history of violence and are not threats to recidivate would appear to be such candidates. Those inmates are usually housed in the BOP's medical centers, which as of December 2012 housed 7,464 inmates.[61] In interviews with BOP staff, we heard anecdotally that the BOP's medical referral centers also are facing capacity issues. For example, the Health Services Administrator at one medical institution told us that his institution has had inadequate bed space and has had to have sick inmates wait 1 to 2 weeks for a bed. He added that he understood wait times at other medical institutions were even longer. In addition, our review of a case file for one inmate who died during consideration found comments from a medical institution staff member that the inmate was not transferred to the medical institution because there was no bed space and that several inmates were on a list ahead of the inmate.

Conclusion

We found that effectively managing the compassionate release program would result in cost savings for the BOP. However, we also found that the BOP does not track marginal daily costs for incarcerating medical inmates, nor does it track costs related to the care and confinement of inmates diagnosed with terminal illnesses or inmates with severely debilitating medical conditions. Therefore, neither the BOP nor the OIG is able to determine the amount spent per inmate for the treatment and care of inmates with terminal illnesses or serious medical conditions. Having such information would allow the BOP to accurately determine the amount spent for such inmates in its medical facilities, the cost of certain medical services for seriously ill and terminal patients, and the cost savings achieved by releasing inmates through the compassionate release program. Finally, we found that effectively managing the compassionate release program also provides the BOP with a significant non-monetary benefit, namely assistance in managing the growing inmate population that has resulted in significant capacity issues for the BOP.

A Small Percentage of Inmates Released under the Program Were Rearrested

According to the BOP's Program Statement, it seeks to operate the compassionate release program in a manner that protects the public from undue risk. We attempted to determine recidivism rates within the compassionate release program by asking the Federal Bureau of Investigation (FBI) for arrest data for the 142 inmates who had been approved and released through the compassionate release program from 2006 through 2011.[62] We then calculated the recidivism rate by searching for dates of re-arrest within 3 years of the dates of release under the program. Based on these parameters, we found that of the 142 inmates approved and released during our 6-year review period, 5 (3.5 percent) were rearrested within a 3-year period.[63] By comparison, the general recidivism rate for federal offenders has been estimated to be 41 percent within 3 years after release.[64]

According to the data obtained through the FBI for these five released inmates, the offenses for which they were rearrested included probation violations, theft, and drug offenses. Below are summaries on the five inmates who were rearrested, including the circumstances that led to the inmates' release and the offenses for which they were rearrested after release.

- Inmate A had been incarcerated after pleading guilty to possession with intent to distribute marijuana and being sentenced to 60 months of imprisonment, to be followed by 3 years of supervised release. The inmate thereafter was diagnosed with metastatic squamous cell cancer of the lung. His condition was determined to be terminal with a life expectancy of less than 6 months at the time of his release. One year after his release the inmate violated the conditions of his supervised release when he was rearrested for using, administering, and possessing illegally obtained prescription medication and methamphetamine. The inmate admitted that he was abusing methamphetamine and illegally obtained prescription medication on a daily basis. The inmate was returned to the BOP's custody for an additional 12-month sentence.

- Inmate B had been incarcerated following convictions for attempted distribution of PCP and distribution of heroin and having been sentenced to 54 months of imprisonment, to be followed by 5 years on supervised release. The inmate thereafter was diagnosed with advanced idiopathic restrictive cardiomyopathy with congestive heart failure. His condition was determined to be terminal with a life expectancy of less than 6 months at the time of release. The inmate was rearrested 2 years after his release for theft (involving less than $100). The FBI data indicates that the charge was thereafter voluntarily dismissed by the prosecutor.
- Inmate C had been incarcerated after pleading guilty to conspiracy to distribute cocaine and cocaine base and being sentenced to 121 months of imprisonment, to be followed by 5 years on supervised release. The inmate thereafter was diagnosed with end-stage HIV/AIDS, insulin-dependent diabetes mellitus, retinopathy, peripheral neuropathy, chronic renal insufficiency with nephrotic syndrome, and dyslipidemia, with an elevation of plasma cholesterol. The inmate's medical condition was considered "grave," with a "limited life expectancy" at the time of release. Twenty months after his release, he was arrested for possession of cocaine with intent to sell, manufacture, or deliver, and operation of a vehicle with unsafe or improper equipment. Forty-one months after his release, the inmate was again arrested for trafficking in cocaine over 28 grams/less than 150 kilograms, disobeying a stop or yield sign, and possession of drug paraphernalia.
- Inmate D had been incarcerated after pleading guilty to unlawful use of a controlled substance while in possession of a firearm and being sentenced to 33 months of imprisonment, to be followed by 2 years on supervised release. The inmate thereafter was diagnosed with stage IV Hodgkin's lymphoma. The inmate's condition was considered extremely poor with a life expectancy of several months at the time of release. The inmate was rearrested 2 months after release for resisting arrest.
- Inmate E was incarcerated after pleading guilty to possession of cocaine base and being sentenced to 108 months of imprisonment, to be followed by 2 years on supervised release.[65] The inmate thereafter was diagnosed with metastatic infiltrating ductal carcinoma of the breast. The inmate's life expectancy at the time of release was less

than 6 months. The inmate was rearrested 6 months after release for malicious destruction of property (valued at less than $500).

Conclusion

When considering the impact of the compassionate release program on public safety, we found the rate of recidivism for inmates approved and released through compassionate release to be low compared with the overall rate of recidivism for federal inmates. The OIG recognizes that releasing inmates through the compassionate release program could result in some increase in the number of inmates who are rearrested after release, particularly if the numbers and types of inmates released under compassionate release authority are expanded. However, recidivism data suggests that, given these prisoners' serious medical conditions, a well-managed compassionate release program can significantly minimize the risk to the public from an inmate's early release from prison.

Conclusion and Recommendations

We concluded that an effectively managed compassionate release program would result in cost savings for the BOP, as well as assist the BOP in managing its continually growing inmate population and the resulting capacity challenges it is facing. We further found that such a program would likely have a relatively low rate of recidivism. However, we found that the existing BOP compassionate release program is poorly managed and that its inconsistent and ad hoc implementation has likely resulted in potentially eligible inmates not being considered for release. It has also likely resulted in terminally ill inmates dying before their requests for compassionate release were decided. Problems with the program's management are concentrated in four areas.

First, the BOP's regulations and Program Statement do not establish appropriate medical and non-medical criteria for compassionate release consideration and do not adequately define "extraordinary and compelling" circumstances that might warrant release. We found institution staff had varying understandings of what extraordinary and compelling circumstances warrant consideration for compassionate release. For example, while we were told that the BOP Central Office will consider compassionate release for an inmate with a life expectancy of 12 months or less, some institution staff we interviewed said they will consider an inmate only if the inmate has a life expectancy of 6 months or less. Further, while the BOP's regulations and Program Statement allow for compassionate release based upon non-medical circumstances, neither provides any guidance for such situations. Moreover, the BOP recently stated that its practice is to deny non-medical compassionate release requests, and indeed we found that the BOP did not approve a single non-medical compassionate release request during the 6-year period covered by our review. While the BOP proposed revisions to its compassionate release regulations to clarify the conditions that qualify for consideration, a final regulation was never adopted. Consequently, BOP staff continues to decide compassionate release requests without clear or comprehensive standards.

Second, the BOP has failed to put in place timeliness standards at each step of the review process. Instead, Wardens are told simply to promptly review requests and to expedite reviews of requests for medical reasons. Not surprisingly, we found that institutions interpret these general directions differently. Not all institutions have a designated timeframe for reviewing requests and, for those that do, the timeframes range from 5 to 65 days.

Third, the BOP does not have procedures to inform inmates about the compassionate release program. Unlike with many other BOP programs, institution staff is not required to inform inmates about the compassionate release program and the methods used by staff that does inform inmates about the program vary by institution. As a result, potentially eligible inmates may not know about the compassionate release program. By making inmates fully aware of the compassionate release program, whether through institution handbooks or during required discussions between inmates and staff, the BOP will be able to increase inmates' knowledge of the program and provide full and fair opportunities for those who may be appropriate for consideration.

Fourth, the BOP does not have a system to track all compassionate release requests, the timeliness of the review process, or whether decisions made by institution and regional office staff are consistent with each other or with BOP policy. As a result, the BOP could not tell us how many requests for compassionate release were made from 2006 through 2011, how many requests were denied by Wardens and how many were denied by Regional Directors, or what the reasons were for those denials. The BOP tracks only inmate requests that have been approved by both the Warden and Regional Director, and that have been sent to the Central Office for review by the BOP Director. We found that some, but not all, institutions and Regional Offices do have their own systems for tracking inmate requests, but that the methods vary. We further found that the BOP Central Office makes no effort to ensure that denial and approval decisions by Wardens and Regional Directors are consistent across institutions and regions, and with BOP policy. We believe that the BOP cannot effectively manage the compassionate release program if it cannot account for the overall number of inmate requests and how they were resolved.

The BOP also does not track the time it takes to process requests and has no formal or standard means of determining the date the review process begins. Consequently, the BOP cannot monitor its process effectively. This is especially problematic for inmates with terminal medical conditions, and we found that 13 percent of inmates whose requests had been approved for compassionate release by a Warden and Regional Director died before a decision was made by the BOP Director. Given the lack of tracking data, we could not assess the timeliness of the review process. While the OIG recognizes the importance of a careful review process, given the time-sensitive nature of compassionate release requests, we believe the BOP should assess the length of time the process takes and establish timeliness standards for each phase of the review process. Clear timeliness standards and a formal mechanism for dating the initiation of the review process will help the BOP determine if delays in the process exist and where to take corrective actions so that the review process may progress as quickly as possible.

Further, the BOP does not maintain cost data associated with the custody and treatment of inmates who may be eligible for compassionate release. Despite this lack of data, the BOP reported to Congress that it could save $3.2 million by expanding the compassionate release program. While appropriately expanding the compassionate release program would inevitably result in medical cost savings, we found that no analysis has been conducted by the BOP. As a result, neither the BOP nor the OIG can determine with any precision the costs associated with providing health care to inmates eligible for compassionate release or the cost savings that could be achieved by releasing such inmates under the program.

Finally, we found the rate of recidivism for inmates approved and released through the existing compassionate release program to be low compared with the overall rate for federal inmates released into the community. While the OIG recognizes that increasing the number of inmates eligible for compassionate release could result in some increase in the number of inmates who are rearrested after release, the recidivism data to date shows that a program that carefully evaluates the risk of releasing an inmate can substantially reduce the likelihood of re-arrest.

Below are our recommendations for improving the compassionate release program.

Recommendations

To ensure that the BOP is effectively and efficiently managing its budget and addressing the growing and significant capacity issues at its institutions:

1) Consider appropriately expanding the use of the compassionate release program as authorized by Congress and as described in the BOP's regulations and Program Statement to cover both medical and non-medical conditions for inmates who do not present a threat to the community and who present a minimal risk of recidivism.

To ensure policies used to consider requests are complete and accurate, we recommend that the BOP:

2) Update written national policies, including its compassionate release regulations and Program Statement, to accurately reflect the BOP's criteria for determining eligible medical and non-medical requests.
3) Provide training for BOP staff responsible for reviewing inmate requests and applying the criteria for evaluating medical and non-medical requests.

To ensure that requests are processed in a timely manner, we recommend that the BOP:

4) Establish timeframes for processing requests at each step of the review process, including Warden, Central Office, and external agency input and review.
5) Establish timeframes for handling inmate appeals that take into account the time sensitivity of compassionate release requests.

To ensure inmates are made aware of the compassionate release program, we recommend that the BOP:

6) Require that all inmates be informed about the compassionate release program, including how to initiate a request and circumstances that may qualify as "extraordinary and compelling."

To ensure the BOP can account for all requests for compassionate release, minimize potential delays in the review process, and ensure denial decisions made by Wardens are appropriate, we recommend that the BOP:

7) Track each compassionate release request, its status, and final disposition.
8) Establish a procedure to formally document the initiation, including the initiation date, for each compassionate release request.
9) Require that Wardens document the specific reasons for denying an inmate's request for compassionate release.
10) Include as part of BOP program compliance reviews an element for reviewing compassionate release determinations made by Wardens.

To accurately determine the costs associated with providing health services to inmates who may be otherwise eligible for compassionate release and identify potential cost savings, we recommend that the BOP:

11) Collect and assess the costs for providing health services to inmates diagnosed with terminal medical conditions and a limited life expectancy, and severely debilitating medical conditions.

APPENDIX I: LEGISLATIVE HISTORY

Sentencing Reform Act of 1984 (Pub. L. No. 98-473, 18 U.S.C. §§ 3551-3556)

The *Sentencing Reform Act of 1984,* Title II of the *Comprehensive Crime Control Act of 1984,* was passed by Congress and signed into law by the President on October 12, 1984. The legislation permits an inmate to petition for a sentence reduction for extraordinary and compelling reasons. According to the *Sentencing Reform Act of 1984,* a court can reduce a prisoner's imprisonment term if the BOP files a motion based on "extraordinary and compelling" reasons.

Under 18 U.S.C. § 3582(c)(1)(A), a sentencing court, on motion of the BOP Director, may reduce the term of imprisonment of an inmate sentenced under the *Comprehensive Crime Control Act of 1984.* The BOP oversees this program in accordance with 18 U.S.C. § 3582(c)(1)(A) and the procedures set forth in 28 C.F.R. § 571.60-.64.

Under 18 U.S.C. § 4205(g), a sentencing court, on motion of the BOP, may make an inmate with a minimum term sentence immediately eligible for parole by reducing the minimum term of the sentence to time served. Effective November 1, 1987, 18 U.S.C. § 4205(g) was repealed, but it remains the controlling law for inmates whose offenses occurred prior to that date. For inmates whose offenses occurred on or after November 1, 1987, the applicable statute is 18 U.S.C. § 3582(c)(1)(A). Procedures for compassionate release of an inmate under either provision are contained in 28 C.F.R. part 571, subpart G.

28 C.F.R. § 571.60-.64

Subsections 571.60-.64 of Title 28 of the C.F.R. establish the purpose and scope, initiation of request, approval of request, denial of request, and ineligible offenders for compassionate release (procedures for the implementation of 18 U.S.C. §§ 3582(c)(1)(A) and 4205(g)):

- § 571.60 (Purpose and scope): Under 18 U.S.C. § 4205(g), a sentencing court, on motion of the BOP, may make an inmate with a minimum term sentence immediately eligible for parole by reducing the minimum term of the sentence to time served. Under 18 U.S.C. § 3582(c)(1)(A), a sentencing court, on motion of the BOP Director, may reduce the term of imprisonment of an inmate sentenced under the *Comprehensive Crime Control Act of 1984.* The BOP uses 18 U.S.C. §§ 4205(g) and 3582(c)(1)(A) in particularly extraordinary or compelling circumstances that could not reasonably have been foreseen by the court at the time of sentencing.
- § 571.61 (Initiation of request – extraordinary or compelling circumstances): A request for a motion under 18 U.S.C. § 4205(g) or § 3582(c)(1)(A) shall be submitted to the Warden. Ordinarily, the request shall be in writing and submitted by the inmate. An inmate may initiate a request for consideration under 18 U.S.C. § 4205(g) or § 3582(c)(1)(A) only when there are particularly extraordinary or

compelling circumstances that could not reasonably have been foreseen by the court at the time of sentencing. The inmate's request shall at a minimum contain the following information:

1) The extraordinary or compelling circumstances that the inmate believes warrant consideration.
2) Proposed release plans, including where the inmate will reside, how the inmate will support him- or herself, and, if the basis for the request involves the inmate's health, information on where the inmate will receive medical treatment and how the inmate will pay for such treatment.

The BOP processes a request made by another person on behalf of an inmate in the same manner as an inmate's request. Staff shall refer a request received at the Central Office or at a Regional Office to the Warden of the institution where the inmate is confined.

- § 571.62 (Approval of request): The BOP makes a motion under 18 U.S.C. § 4205(g) or § 3582(c)(1)(A) only after the request has been reviewed by the Warden, the Regional Director, the General Counsel, and either the Medical Director for medical referrals or the Assistant Director, Correctional Programs Division, for nonmedical referrals, and with the approval of the BOP Director. The Warden shall promptly review a request for consideration under 18 U.S.C. § 4205(g) or § 3582(c)(1)(A). If the Warden, upon an investigation of the request determines that the request warrants approval, the Warden shall refer the matter in writing with a recommendation to the Regional Director. If the Regional Director determines that the request warrants approval, the Regional Director shall prepare a written recommendation and refer the matter to the Office of General Counsel. If the General Counsel determines that the request warrants approval, the General Counsel shall solicit the opinion of either the Medical Director or the Assistant Director, Correctional Programs Division, depending upon the nature of the basis of the request. With this opinion, the General Counsel shall forward the entire matter to the BOP Director for final decision. If the BOP Director grants a request under 18 U.S.C. § 4205(g), the Director will contact the U.S. Attorney in the district in which the inmate was sentenced regarding filing a motion in the sentencing court on behalf of the BOP to reduce the minimum term of the inmate's sentence to time served. If the BOP

Director grants a request under 18 U.S.C. § 3582(c)(1)(A), the Director will contact the U.S. Attorney in the district in which the inmate was sentenced regarding filing a motion in the sentencing court on behalf of the BOP Director to reduce the inmate's term of imprisonment to time served. Upon receipt of notice that the sentencing court has entered an order granting the motion under 18 U.S.C. § 4205(g), the Warden of the institution where the inmate is confined shall schedule the inmate for hearing on the earliest Parole Commission docket. Upon receipt of notice that the sentencing court has entered an order granting the motion under 18 U.S.C. § 3582(c)(1)(A), the Warden of the institution where the inmate is confined shall release the inmate forthwith. In the event the basis of the request is the medical condition of the inmate, staff shall expedite the request at all levels.

- § 571.63 (Denial of request): When an inmate's request is denied by the Warden or Regional Director, the official shall provide the inmate with a written notice and statement of reasons for the denial. The inmate may appeal the denial through the administrative remedy procedure (28 C.F.R. part 542, subpart B). When an inmate's request for consideration under 18 U.S.C. § 4205(g) or § 3582(c)(1)(A) is denied by the Director or the General Counsel, the General Counsel shall provide the inmate with a written notice and statement of reasons for the denial. This denial constitutes a final administrative decision, and an inmate may not appeal the denial through the administrative remedy procedure.
- § 571.64 (Ineligible offenders): The BOP has no authority to initiate a request under 18 U.S.C. § 4205(g) or § 3582(c)(1)(A) on behalf of state prisoners housed in BOP facilities or D.C. Code offenders confined in federal institutions. The BOP cannot initiate such a motion on behalf of federal offenders who committed their offenses prior to November 1, 1987, and received non-parolable sentences.

U.S. Sentencing Commission Guidelines

Effective November 1, 2007, and pursuant to 28 U.S.C. § 994(p), the U.S. Sentencing Commission (USSC) amended he sentencing guidelines to describe what should be considered extraordinary and compelling reasons for sentence reduction (compassionate release), including criteria to be applied.

The USSC guidelines provide four examples of circumstances that, provided the defendant is not a danger to the safety of any other person or to the community, would constitute "extraordinary and compelling reasons" for purposes of 18 U.S.C. § 3582(c)(1)(A). According to the USSC guidelines, extraordinary and compelling reasons exist when:

1) The defendant is suffering from a terminal illness.
2) The defendant is suffering from a permanent physical or medical condition, or is experiencing deteriorating physical or mental health because of the aging process, that substantially diminishes the ability of the defendant to provide self-care and for which conventional treatment promises no substantial improvement.
3) The death or incapacitation of the defendant's only family member capable of caring for the defendant's minor child or minor children.
4) Any other circumstance that the Director of the Bureau of Prisons finds to be an extraordinary and compelling reason.

Department Component Policy

BOP Director Memorandum

On July 22, 1994, the BOP Director issued a memorandum to BOP executive staff regarding compassionate release requests. The memorandum indicated that the BOP took a conservative approach to filing motions for compassionate release, and that the BOP had been considering for release only those inmates with a terminal illness and a life expectancy of 6 months or less. The memorandum noted that the BOP had recently extended this time limit to include those inmates with a life expectancy of up to 1 year and stated that the time limit was a general guideline, not a requirement. The memorandum also stated that there may be cases where an inmate may not have a terminal condition or limited life expectancy, but has a serious or debilitating medical condition, and that those circumstances may merit consideration. In addition, the memorandum stated that each case must be judged on an individual basis, and provided factors for staff to consider when evaluating cases. Those factors included:

- the nature and circumstances of the offense;
- the age of the inmate,
- the danger, if any, the inmate poses to the public if released,

- appropriate release plans, including family or outside resources,
- the nature and severity of the inmate's illness, including whether outside medical care will be necessary, and
- the length of the inmate's sentence and the amount of time left to serve.

The memorandum stated that the factors listed above were not criteria that an inmate must meet to be considered for compassionate release. Rather, the factors were guidelines to be evaluated before staff made a final decision on an inmate's request.

BOP Program Statement 5050.46

The BOP's Program Statement, Compassionate Release, Procedures for Implementation of 18 U.S.C. §§ 3582(c)(1)(A) and 4205(g), last revised on May 19, 1998, establishes policies and procedures for submitting and reviewing compassionate release requests, and includes processes for considering both medical and non-medical requests. The Program Statement includes the purpose and scope of the statutes establishing compassionate release, as well as the objectives of the program. The program's objectives include:

- a motion for a modification of a sentence will be made to the sentencing court only in particularly extraordinary or compelling circumstances that could not reasonably have been foreseen by the court at the time of sentencing,
- the public will be protected from undue risk by careful review of each compassionate release request, and
- compassionate release motions will be filed with the sentencing judge in accordance with the statutory requirements of 18 U.S.C. § 3582(c)(1)(A).

The Program Statement also includes procedures for initiating a request. Specifically, a request for a motion for compassionate release shall be submitted by the inmate to the Warden, ordinarily in writing, only when there are particularly extraordinary and compelling circumstances that the inmate believes could not reasonably have been foreseen by the court at the time of sentencing. An inmate must also provide a proposed release plan when submitting a request. The BOP processes a request made by a person on behalf of the inmate in the same manner as an inmate's request.

Also, the Program Statement establishes the process for approving requests. The Program Statement states that the BOP makes a motion for compassionate release only after review of the request by the Warden, the Regional Director, the General Counsel, and either the Medical Director (for medical requests), or the Assistant Director of the Correctional Programs Division (for non-medical requests). Requests must be approved by the BOP Director.

In addition, the Program Statement states that if a request is denied by the Warden, Regional Director, or General Counsel, the disapproving official must provide the inmate with written notice and a statement of reasons for the denial. The inmate may appeal a denial made by the Warden or Regional Director through the BOP's administrative remedy procedure. However, the inmate may not appeal a denial by the General Counsel as the denial constitutes a final administrative decision. If the Director denies the inmate's request, the inmate is provided a written notice and a statement of reasons for the denial within 20 workdays after receipt of the referral from the BOP's Office of General Counsel. A denial by the Director also constitutes a final administrative decision and cannot by be appealed by the inmate.

Finally, the Program Statement clarifies offenders who are ineligible for compassionate release. The procedures contained in the Program Statement are the same as those established in 28 C.F.R. § 571.61-.64.

APPENDIX II: METHODOLOGY OF THE OIG REVIEW

We reviewed the BOP's process to approve or deny inmate requests for compassionate release. We reviewed federal laws and regulations; BOP Program Statements; BOP and USAO policies and procedures; and written correspondence of recommendations between BOP, USAO, and the Department and component officials. We conducted case file reviews of all inmates whose requests for compassionate release were approved or denied by the BOP's Director, or who died during the BOP's consideration of their requests. We also sent a questionnaire to all BOP Wardens to evaluate the processes and procedures institutions use to consider inmate requests for compassionate release. In addition, we interviewed Department officials with the BOP, EOUSA, ODAG, and USAOs, as well as staff at three BOP institutions. Finally, we conducted videoconference site visits with three BOP institutions. The following sections provide additional information on the methodology of our review.

Data Analysis

Case File Review

We conducted case file reviews of all inmates, from 2006 through 2011, whose request for compassionate release was approved or denied by the BOP Director, or who died during the BOP's consideration of their requests. The BOP provided the OIG with 212 case files for inmates whose requests were received by the BOP's Office of General Counsel after approval by the Wardens and Regional Directors. We reviewed 208 case files in which a decision to approve or deny was made, or the inmate died before a decision. We received one duplicate case file for an inmate. In addition, we did not review the case files for three inmates who did not receive a decision, including one inmate whose sentence was vacated by the court, one inmate who withdrew the request, and one inmate whose case was referred for a criminal matter.

The purpose of our case file review was multi-faceted. First, we obtained inmate demographic information. Second, we reviewed the steps of the review process, including which institutions initiated requests, and attempted to obtain dates for the initiation of a request and completion of steps throughout the consideration process. These include the date a request was initiated, dates institution staff received feedback from outside agencies, and the date the Warden approved the request. Third, we analyzed documents and BOP correspondence with institution and Central Office staff, USAOs, and law enforcement agencies. Finally, we reviewed documents to determine why an inmate's request was approved or denied by the BOP Director.

Questionnaire

We e-mailed a questionnaire to all BOP Wardens. The purpose of our questionnaire was to evaluate the procedures institutions use to consider inmate requests for compassionate release.

Our questionnaire included 10 questions. Specifically, we asked Wardens about how inmates were made aware of the program; the most common method inmates use to submit requests; who reviews requests for compassionate release; the approximate number of requests their institution received over the past 2 calendar years, including the number of requests for non-medical reasons; the number of non-medical requests approved by their institution; and what factors the Wardens consider during their reviews of requests to make a determination. Further, we asked Wardens if their institutions had designated timeframes for reviewing requests, and if so, to specify those timeframes; and whether their institutions tracks requests. Finally, we asked Wardens to describe the process they and their staff use to review requests, resources available to consider requests for medical reasons, and if they had recommendations to improve the process for considering requests.

We received 100 responses from institution Wardens. Ten of the Wardens responded on behalf of multiple institutions within a Federal Correctional Complex (FCC). An FCC contains multiple institutions with different missions and security levels located in close proximity to one another. Because in 10 cases a singular response from a Warden represented multiple institutions within a FCC, the 100 responses we received represented 110 of the 117 (94 percent) BOP institutions.

Document Analysis

We reviewed the laws, regulations, and legislative history of the compassionate release program. We also reviewed BOP Program Statements, training materials, correspondence between the BOP's Central Office and institutions, and USAO documents. In addition, we examined BOP internal memoranda, evaluative guidelines, and criteria for medical requests.

Interviews

Organization/Division	Position
Office of the Deputy Attorney General	
	Associate Deputy Attorney General
	Senior Counsel to the Deputy Attorney General
Federal Bureau of Prisons	
BOP Headquarters	Director
	Regional Directors (x6)
	Assistant Director, Correctional Programs Division
	Assistant Director and General Counsel
	Assistant Director and Medical Director
	Senior Deputy General Counsel
	Administrator, Correctional Programs Division
	Senior Counsel (x2)
	Senior Deputy Assistant Director, Administration Division
	Assistant General Counsel (x3)
	Chief, Office of Legislative Affairs (x2)
	Social Science Research Analyst
FPC Alderson	Warden

Organization/Division	Position
	Associate Warden
	Case Management Coordinator
	Unit Manager
	Medical Officer
	Case Manager
FMC Butner	Warden
	Associate Warden
	Social Worker and Chairperson of the Reduction in Sentence (Compassionate Release) Review Committee
	Oncologist and Tumor Board Chairperson
	Social Worker
	Case Manager
FMC Carswell	Warden
	Associate Warden
	Health Services Administrator
	Social Worker and Chairperson of Compassionate Release Review Committee
	Director of Nursing
	Chief Social Worker
	Unit Manager
	Case Manager
Executive Office for the United States Attorneys	
	Counsel for Legal Initiatives
United States Attorneys' Offices	
	Criminal Chief, Southern District of Florida
	Criminal Chief, Southern District of Texas
	Criminal Chief, Eastern District of Michigan
	Criminal Chief, Southern District of Iowa
	Criminal Chief, Eastern District of Oklahoma
	Criminal Chief, Eastern District of Kentucky
	Assistant United States Attorney, Western District of Texas
	Assistant United States Attorney, Southern District of Indiana

Video Teleconferences

All interviews with BOP institution staff were conducted through video teleconferencing (VTC). The team conducted VTCs with three institutions: Federal Prison Camp (FPC) Alderson, Federal Medical Center (FMC) Butner, and FMC Carswell. We choose FMC Butner and FMC Carswell because they received the highest number of compassionate release requests, based on our case file review. FPC Alderson was randomly selected from 103 institutions that, based on our case file review, received no requests in 2011.

Appendix III: Former BOP Director Memorandum

U.S. Department of Justice

Federal Bureau of Prisons

Office of the Director

Washington, DC 20534

July 22, 1994

MEMORANDUM FOR EXECUTIVE STAFF

FROM: Kathleen M. Hawk, Director
Federal Bureau of Prisons

SUBJECT: Compassionate Release Requests

The Bureau of Prisons has historically taken a conservative approach to filing a motion with the courts for the compassionate release of an inmate under 18 U.S.C. § 4205(g) or § 3582(c)(1)(A). Until recently, our general guideline was to recommend release of an inmate only in cases of terminal illness when life expectancy was six months or less. Not many months ago, we extended the time limit to a one year life expectancy as long as medical staff felt comfortable with the accuracy of their prediction of life expectancy. Of course, this is a general guideline, not a requirement.

As we have further reviewed this issue, it has come to our attention that there may be other cases that merit consideration for release. These cases still fall within the medical arena, but may not be terminal or lend themselves to a precise prediction of life expectancy. Nevertheless, such cases may be extremely serious and debilitating.

While each case must be judged on an individual basis, with consideration of a number of factors, we are willing to consider other cases for possible recommendation for release. In evaluating individual cases that you may wish to submit, you and your staff should consider and balance the following factors, in addition to others that may bear on your recommendation:

- the nature and circumstances of the offense (e.g., was violence or a weapon used);

- the criminal and personal history and characteristics of the inmate, including an assessment of whether the inmate is likely to participate in criminal activities if released (Does the inmate have other criminal convictions?);

- the age of the inmate (both current age and age at time of sentencing);

- the danger, if any, the inmate poses to the public if released (Does the inmate have a history of violence? Could the inmate still commit his/her prior offense even in his/her present condition?);

- appropriate release plans, including family or outside resources (Does the inmate have insurance or the ability to pay for necessary medical care? If released, would the cost of care be borne by taxpayers?);

- the nature and severity of the inmate's illness, including consideration of whether outside medical care will be necessary; for example:

    - an inmate with severe debilitating heart or kidney disease that clearly limits his or her daily activity and in which conventional treatment such as medication, dialysis, or other measures are not sufficient to stabilize the disease or illness;

    - an inmate with a terminal illness, but no definitive life expectancy can be determined.

  Cases which could be remedied with transplantation will be considered, but other factors such as time remaining on the inmate's sentence will be weighed heavily to determine if a release motion is appropriate;

- the length of the inmate's sentence and the amount of time left to serve.

'hese factors are not criteria which the inmate must meet to ualify for consideration; rather, they are guidelines which hould be evaluated before staff make a final decision. Staff hould not recommend compassionate release merely because the nmate has met a majority of the above factors. Instead, staff hould rely on their correctional judgment, available ocumentation, and verifiable information in making ecommendations.

f: OGC - LCI
File - Exec Staff, OGC

APPENDIX IV: TALKING POINTS PREPARED FOR PRESENTATIONS BY THE BOP'S GENERAL COUNSEL TO WARDENS AND OTHER BOP STAFF

The following was provided by the BOP and presented verbatim by the OIG.

I. Legal Authority and Procedures

a) 18 U.S.C. § 3582(c)(1)(A)(i), gives the BOP Director the statutory authority and discretion to motion the sentencing court to reduce an inmate's term of imprisonment in extraordinary or compelling circumstances.

b) The BOP only exercises this authority when the "extraordinary and compelling circumstances" involve an inmate who is suffering from a life-threatening or terminal medical condition, or who is severely and permanently mentally or physically debilitated.

c) Procedurally, in accordance with BOP policy and 28 C.F.R. § 571.60 et seq.:
   - An inmate or an inmate's family or representative may initiate a RIS request at the institution level.
   - If the Warden determines that a RIS is warranted, the Warden will forward a written recommendation together with the RIS package to the Regional Director.
   - If the Regional Director agrees that a RIS is warranted, the Regional Director will forward a written recommendation together with the RIS package to the Office of General Counsel.
   - If the General Counsel, after obtaining a medical recommendation from the Medical Director, agrees that a RIS is warranted, legal staff prepare a draft Motion and Order, and a letter for the Director's signature requesting that the U.S. Attorney in the sentencing jurisdiction submit the Motion for a RIS to the sentencing court.
   - If the Director agrees that the RIS is warranted, she will sign the letter and forward it, together with the draft Motion, and Order to the US Attorney's Office.

- The inmate may appeal the Warden's or Regional Director's denial through the administrative remedy process.

II. Expanded Medical Criteria for Reduction in Sentence

1) Terminal illness (with a life expectancy of one year or less); or
2) Severely physically or cognitively debilitated which significantly impairs physical and/or mental function and will not improve with treatment seriously limits daily activities.

III. Guidelines for Inmate Eligibility for a Reduction in Sentence (RIS)

A. If an inmate meets the medical criteria for RIS consideration, staff should rely on all available documents, correctional judgment, and verifiable information when making a recommendation for RIS. Staff should consider:

- the nature and circumstances of the offense. E.g., Was violence or a weapon involved in the offense?
- the criminal and personal history, and characteristics of the inmate. E.g., Are there other criminal convictions that are serious or share similar characteristics?
- the likelihood the inmate will participate in criminal activities if released.
- the inmate's current age, age at the time of sentencing, and whether the inmate could still commit his/her offense in his/her current medical condition.
- whether the court likely knew or foresaw, based on the inmate's age and medical history or condition at the time of sentencing, that the inmate would probably die before completing his/her sentence.
- the danger, if any, the inmate poses to the public or himself/herself if released. Does the inmate have a history of violence?
- the length of the sentence and the amount of time left to serve on the sentence.
- appropriateness of the release plan. E.g., Does the inmate have an adequate support system including family, financial, and medical resources?

IV. Sentencing Commission Guidelines Amendment 1B1.13

A. Effective November 1, 2007, for these amendments.

- Extraordinary and Compelling Reasons.
- The defendant is suffering from a terminal illness.
- The defendant is suffering from a permanent physical or medical condition, or is experiencing deteriorating physical or mental health because of the aging process, that substantially diminishes the ability of the defendant to provide self-care within the environment of a correctional facility and for which conventional treatment promises no substantial improvement.
- The death or incapacitation of the defendant's only family member capable of caring for the defendant's minor child or minor children.
- As determined by the Director of the BOP, there exists in the defendant's case an extraordinary and compelling reason other than, or in combination with, the reasons described in subdivisions (i), (ii), and (iii).
- Do not summarily deny cases that fall within these guideline parameters but outside BOP criteria. Denials of these requests should address these issues but stay within BOP medical criteria.
- Contact legal counsel in the CLC, Regional Office, or Central Office for assistance.

APPENDIX V: REQUEST DECISIONS

From 2006 through 2011, Wardens and Regional Directors approved and forwarded 211 inmate requests to the BOP's Central Office for review.[66] The BOP Director considered those requests and approved 142 (68 percent) and denied 38 (18 percent). We also found that in 28 (13 percent) cases, the inmates died while their requests were being considered by the BOP's Central Office and before a decision was made by the BOP Director. Table 2 shows the number of requests forwarded to the BOP's Central Office by Wardens and Regional Directors from 2006 through 2011, and the number of those requests that were approved and denied by the BOP Director, as well as the number of inmates who died while their requests were being considered by the BOP's Central Office.

Table 2. Requests Approved and Denied by the BOP's Central Office and Inmates who Died Before a Decision, 2006 through 2011

Year	Approved	Denied	Died Before Decision
2006	28	10	5
2007	16	10	4
2008	27	3	7
2009	17	5	3
2010	25	6	7
2011	29	4	2
Total	142	38	28

Source: BOP.

Of the requests received by the BOP's Central Office that we reviewed, we found that 206 requests (99 percent) were for medical reasons and 2 requests (1 percent) were for non-medical reasons. Of the 142 requests approved by the BOP Director, 118 requests (83 percent) were because the inmates had terminal medical conditions and limited life expectancy, and 24 requests (17 percent) were for severely debilitating medical conditions. Table 3 shows the reasons requests were approved by the BOP Director from 2006 through 2011.

Table 3. Reasons Requests Were Approved, 2006 through 2011

Year	Requests	Terminal Illness and Limited Life Expectancy	Debilitating Conditions
2006	28	24	4
2007	16	14	2
2008	27	23	4
2009	17	14	3
2010	25	21	4
2011	29	22	7
Total	142	118	24

Source: BOP.

Of the 38 requests denied by the BOP's Director, 22 (58 percent) were due to the seriousness of the inmate's offense or criminal history, 8 (21 percent) were because the inmate's circumstances did not meet the BOP's medical criteria, 1 (3 percent) was because the court knew about the inmate's circumstances at the time of sentencing, and 7 (18 percent) were a combination of these factors. Table 4 shows the reasons requests were denied by the BOP's Director from 2006 through 2011.

Table 4. Reasons Requests Were Denied, 2006 through 2011

Year	Requests	Seriousness of Offense or Criminal History	Did Not Meet Medical Criteria	Court Aware of Condition During Sentencing	Combination
2006	10	7	1	0	2
2007	10	8	2	0	0
2008	3	2	0	0	1
2009	5	2	2	0	1
2010	6	2	2	0	2
2011	4	1	1	1	1
Totals	38	22	8	1	7

Source: BOP.

APPENDIX VI: FEDERAL BUREAU OF PRISONS' RESPONSE TO DRAFT REPORT

U.S. Department of Justice

Federal Bureau of Prisons

Office of the Director

Washington, DC 20534

April 17, 2013

MEMORANDUM FOR SARAH E. BATIPPS
DIRECTOR, EVALUATION AND INSPECTIONS
OFFICE OF INSPECTOR GENERAL

THRU: Thomas R. Kane
Deputy Director
Federal Bureau of Prisons

FROM: Charles E. Samuels, Jr.
Director
Federal Bureau of Prisons

SUBJECT: Response to the Office of Inspector General's Draft Report - The Federal Bureau of Prisons' Compassionate Release Program

The Bureau of Prisons (BOP or Bureau) appreciates the opportunity to comment upon the Office of the Inspector General (OIG) above-referenced draft report as well as to respond to the recommendations directed at the BOP. Please find below the recommendations directed at the Bureau and the Bureau's response to each recommendation. For the reasons set forth below, we respectfully request that Recommendations 5 and 11 be closed at this time.

OIG Recommendation #1: Consider appropriately expanding the use of the compassionate release program as authorized by Congress and as described in the BOP's regulations and Program Statement to cover both medical and non-medical conditions for inmates who do not present a threat to the community and who present a minimal risk of recidivism.

BOP Response: As the BOP has advised OIG, the Bureau is already in the process of reviewing and modifying aspects of the compassionate release program. The BOP plans to issue new guidance on medical criteria to consider in determining whether a request based on underlying medical circumstances is "extraordinary and compelling" to warrant a compassionate release motion to a sentencing judge. Additionally, the BOP has already started a process to consider the subject of non-medical compassionate release.

OIG Recommendation #2: Update written national policies, including its compassionate release regulations and Program Statement, to accurately reflect the BOP's criteria for determining eligible medical and non-medical requests.

BOP Response: The BOP concurs with this recommendation. As noted above, the BOP plans to issue a guidance memorandum that will clarify criteria to be considered in reviewing medical requests until the revised compassionate release regulations and Program Statement are finalized. Additionally, as your report notes, the BOP is already in the process of revising its regulations and Program Statement. Changes to policy in the Program Statement will need to be negotiated with the union. Changes to the regulations will need to go through formal notice and comment procedures.

OIG Recommendation #3: Provide training for BOP staff responsible for reviewing inmate requests and applying the criteria for evaluating medical and non-medical requests.

BOP Response: The BOP concurs with this recommendation. Training will be provided to staff. However, given budget limitations, training may be provided in an on-line and/or video conference format.

OIG Recommendation #4: Establish timeframes for processing requests at each step of the review process, including Warden, Central Office, and external agency input and review.

BOP Response: The BOP concurs in part with this recommendation. BOP agrees that general guidelines for reviewing a request should be established. However, any time frame will need to be flexible so that the specific circumstances of each case can be thoroughly assessed and considered (e.g., if additional time is needed to establish an appropriate release plan for an inmate).

OIG Recommendation #5: Establish timeframes for handling inmate appeals that take into account the time sensitivity of compassionate release requests.

BOP Response: The BOP requests this recommendation be closed. We concur that inmate appeals should be expedited. However, current regulations concerning administrative remedies already provide for expedited processing in certain circumstances. 28 C.F.R. §542.18 states in pertinent part, " . . . [i]f the Request is determined to be of an emergency nature which threatens the inmate's immediate health or welfare, the Warden shall respond not later than the third calendar day after filing. . . ." Accordingly, BOP will now advise staff to use this provision for time sensitive compassionate release requests based on underlying terminal medical conditions. Instruction to staff to utilize this provision in these circumstances will be provided during staff training sessions noted in our response to OIG Recommendation #3.

OIG Recommendation #6: Require that all inmates be informed about the compassionate release program, including how to initiate a request and circumstances that may qualify as "extraordinary and compelling."

BOP Response: The BOP concurs with this recommendation. The Bureau already provides information about the compassionate release program to inmates through the electronic law library. In addition, the BOP plans to provide information relating to its new medical guidance on the Inmate Electronic Bulletin Board. The BOP is already developing a standardized Admissions and Orientation Handbook (A&O Handbook) to be used at all of the Bureau's institutions. BOP plans to include information about compassionate release in the new A&O Handbook.

OIG Recommendation #7: Track each compassionate release request, its status, and final disposition.

BOP Response: The BOP concurs with this recommendation. The BOP is currently working to develop an electronic tracking system to address this recommendation. The BOP anticipates that the electronic tracking system will go live by September 30, 2013.

OIG Recommendation #8: Establish a procedure to formally document the initiation, including the initiation date, for each compassionate release request.

BOP Response: The BOP concurs with this recommendation. As noted in response to OIG Recommendation #7, the BOP is currently working to develop an electronic tracking system to track data related to all compassionate release requests. The BOP will also provide training to staff on procedures to use when inputting information to the electronic tracking system. The BOP plans to incorporate these procedures into its revised Program Statement.

OIG Recommendation #9: Require that Wardens document the specific reasons for denying an inmate's request for compassionate release.

BOP Response: The BOP concurs with this recommendation. The new electronic tracking system procedures will require Wardens to provide the reason for denying an inmate's compassionate release request.

OIG Recommendation #10: Include as part of BOP program compliance reviews an element for reviewing compassionate release determinations made by Wardens.

BOP Response: The BOP concurs with this recommendation. Compliance reviews involving compassionate release will affect several disciplines at the institution level (e.g., Unit Management, Correctional Services, Health Services, etc.). The BOP will review its program review policies to ensure guideline steps, by discipline, are incorporated into existing Program Review Guidelines.

OIG Recommendation #11: Collect and assess the costs for providing health services to inmates diagnosed with terminal medical conditions and a limited life expectancy, and severely debilitating medical conditions.

BOP Response: The BOP concurs in part with this recommendation. The BOP believes it would be time and labor intensive to attempt to calculate medical costs for all inmates who have been diagnosed with terminal medical conditions and a limited life expectancy, and non-terminal medical conditions. Further, these costs will likely vary in each individual case depending on the intensity of medical and custodial care needed over time, the unpredictable nature of an inmate's medical condition and costs of medical treatment over the course of care, and the area of the country the care is being provided, among other factors. Any calculations would have to be based on estimates and average costs. Despite these limitations, BOP concurs that tracking an estimated cost savings for inmates for whom the BOP submitted a compassionate release motion to the sentencing judge and the judge granted early release could be useful. Therefore, the BOP will use the current Actual Annual Cost of Incarceration Rate for each BOP Medical Referral Center and calculate the estimated cost avoidance related to each BOP approved compassionate release case for which the inmate is ultimately released. Accordingly, we request this recommendation be closed.

If you have any questions regarding this response, please contact Sara M. Revell, Assistant Director, Program Review Division, at (202) 353-2302.

APPENDIX VII: OIG ANALYSIS OF FEDERAL BUREAU OF PRISONS' RESPONSE

The Office of the Inspector General provided a draft of this report to the Federal Bureau of Prisons for its comment. The BOP's response is included in Appendix VI to this report. The OIG's analysis of the BOP's response and the actions necessary to close the recommendations are discussed below. Please provide requested information and documentation by July 31, 2013.

Recommendation 1

Consider appropriately expanding the use of the compassionate release program as authorized by Congress and as described in the BOP's regulations and Program Statement to cover both medical and non-medical conditions for inmates who do not present a threat to the community and who present a minimal risk of recidivism.

Status: Resolved.

BOP Response: The BOP concurred with this recommendation, stating that it is in the process of reviewing and modifying aspects of the compassionate release program and plans to issue new guidance on medical criteria to consider in determining whether a request based on underlying medical circumstances is "extraordinary and compelling" to warrant a compassionate release motion to a sentencing judge. The BOP stated it had already started a process to consider the subject of nonmedical compassionate release.

OIG Analysis: The BOP's actions are responsive to this recommendation. As discussed throughout the report, the BOP verbally told the OIG, but did not provide copies, of the new guidance memorandum for medical institutions that will expand the compassionate release program by making inmates with a life expectancy of up to 18 months eligible for consideration. The BOP told the OIG that the new memorandum is also intended to assist staff who review compassionate release requests in understanding what level of functioning is sufficiently "extraordinary and compelling" for inmates with debilitating medical conditions to be considered for release. Please provide the OIG with a copy of the new approved guidance on medical criteria for medical institutions, a description of how the BOP plans to further modify other aspects of the compassionate release program, and actions taken to consider non-medical requests for compassionate release.

Recommendation 2

Update written national policies, including its compassionate release regulations and Program Statement, to accurately reflect the BOP's criteria for determining eligible medical and nonmedical requests.

Status: Resolved.

BOP Response: The BOP concurred with this recommendation, stating that the BOP plans to issue a guidance memorandum that will clarify criteria to be considered in reviewing medical requests until the revised compassionate release regulations and Program Statement are finalized. The BOP stated that it has already started the process of revising its regulations and Program Statement. Changes to policy in the Program Statement will need to be negotiated with the union, and changes to the regulations will need to go through formal notice and comment procedures.

OIG Analysis: The BOP's actions are responsive to this recommendation. However, as discussed on page 26 of this report, the BOP's General Counsel explained that the process to revise the Program Statement could take about 2 years after new regulations are adopted due to the requirement that the BOP negotiate changes to the Program Statement with its union. We are concerned about such a lengthy potential delay in issuing a revised Program Statement given the lack of guidance in the existing Program Statement. While we believe the new guidance the BOP verbally discussed with the OIG will benefit staff at the BOP's medical institutions when considering medical requests for compassionate release, staff and inmates at all BOP institutions should be provided with the most current guidance regarding the compassionate release program. Given the time-sensitive nature of these requests, efforts must be made to expedite the process to finalize and issue revised regulations and the Program Statement. Please provide the OIG with copies of the revised regulations and Program Statement, as well as a timeline for finalizing and issuing the revised regulations and Program Statement.

Recommendation 3

Provide training for BOP staff responsible for reviewing inmate requests and applying the criteria for evaluating medical and non-medical requests.

Status: Resolved.

BOP Response: The BOP concurred with this recommendation, stating that it will provide training to staff, but that due to budget limitations, training may be provided in an online or video conference format.

OIG Analysis: The BOP's planned action is responsive to this recommendation. However, given the lack of guidance in the existing Program Statement, we believe any training provided to staff must reflect the most current guidance, including any guidance provided in the new memorandum discussed throughout this report. In addition, training must be revised to reflect any changes resulting from ongoing revisions to the BOP's regulations and Program Statement regarding compassionate release. Please provide the OIG a copy of training provided to staff.

Recommendation 4

Establish timeframes for processing requests at each step of the review process, including Warden, Central Office, and external agency input and review.

Status: Resolved.

BOP Response: The BOP partially concurred with this recommendation, stating that it agreed that general guidelines for reviewing a request should be established, but that any timeframe will need to be flexible so that the specific circumstances of each case can be thoroughly assessed and considered, such as if additional time is needed to establish an appropriate release plan for an inmate.

OIG Analysis: The BOP's response is partially responsive to this recommendation in that the BOP agrees to establish general guidelines for reviewing requests. As stated in the report, the OIG recognizes the complexity and importance of the compassionate release review process. However, given the time-sensitive nature of these requests, particularly for inmates with terminal medical conditions and limited life expectancies, establishing timeframes and assessing the length of time the process takes for each phase of the review process will enable the BOP to determine if delays in the process exist and where to take corrective actions so that the review process may progress as quickly as possible. Please provide the OIG with the general guidelines the BOP plans to implement at each step of the review process that take into account the time-sensitive nature of compassionate release requests.

Recommendation 5

Establish timeframes for handling inmate appeals that take into account the time sensitivity of compassionate release requests.

Status: Resolved.

BOP Response: The BOP concurred with this recommendation, stating that inmate appeals should be expedited. However, the BOP stated that current regulations concerning administrative remedies already provide for expedited processing in certain circumstances. The BOP referenced 28 C.F.R. § 542.18, which states, ". . . [i]f the Request is determined to be of an emergency nature which threatens the inmate's immediate health or welfare, the Warden shall respond not later than the third calendar day after filing . . . ." The BOP stated that staff will be advised to use this provision for time-sensitive compassionate release requests based on underlying terminal medical conditions and that instruction to staff to use this provision in these circumstances will be provided during staff training sessions noted in its response to Recommendation 3. The BOP requested that this recommendation be closed.

OIG Analysis: The BOP's planned action is partially responsive to this recommendation in that it agrees inmate appeals should be expedited. While the OIG agrees that training to advise staff to use the provision established in 28 C.F.R. § 542.18 for compassionate release requests based on underlying terminal medical conditions will be helpful, the BOP's response did not acknowledge the role of a Regional Director or General Counsel in the inmate appeals process. As noted on page 4 of this report, the BOP published an interim rule that expedited the compassionate release process by removing the Regional Director level of review. However, the BOP's administrative remedy program still requires review by the Regional Director and the General Counsel for an inmate to seek formal review (appeal) by high-level BOP officials of an issue relating to any aspect of his or her incarceration, including any aspect of a compassionate release request. As discussed on page 41, we found that in some cases a Regional Director and the General Counsel took over 100 days to respond to inmate appeals regarding compassionate release. Please provide the OIG a status update that includes the roles of a Regional Director and General Counsel when establishing timeframes for handling inmate appeals that take into account the time sensitivity of compassionate release requests.

Recommendation 6

Require that all inmates be informed about the compassionate release program, including how to initiate a request and circumstances that may qualify as "extraordinary and compelling."

Status: Resolved.

BOP Response: The BOP concurred with this recommendation, stating that the BOP plans to provide information relating to its new medical guidance on the Inmate Electronic Bulletin Board. The BOP also said it is developing a standardized Admissions and Orientation Handbook (A&O Handbook) to be used at all BOP institutions and that the BOP plans to include information about compassionate release in the new A&O Handbook.

OIG Analysis: The BOP's planned actions are responsive to this recommendation. Please provide the OIG with a screenshot of the new medical guidance provided on the Inmate Electronic Bulletin Board, as well as a copy of the new standardized A&O Handbook with the information about compassionate release.

Recommendation 7

Track each compassionate release request, its status, and final disposition.

Status: Resolved.

BOP Response: The BOP concurred with this recommendation, stating that it is developing an electronic tracking system. The BOP stated that it anticipates the electronic tracking system will go live by September 30, 2013.

OIG Analysis: The BOP's planned action is responsive to this recommendation. Please provide the OIG with a screenshot of the electronic tracking system and a description of data to be collected.

Recommendation 8

Establish a procedure to formally document the initiation, including the initiation date, for each compassionate release request.

Status: Resolved.

BOP Response: The BOP concurred with this recommendation, stating that it will provide training to staff on procedures to input information into the electronic tracking system discussed in response to Recommendation 7. The BOP also stated that it plans to incorporate these procedures into its revised Program Statement.

OIG Analysis: The BOP's planned actions are responsive to this recommendation. Please provide the OIG with a screenshot of the electronic tracking system that indicates how the initiation of a compassionate release request will be formally documented and a description of the procedures for formally documenting the initiation of each request that the BOP plans to use in staff training and to incorporate into the revised Program Statement.

Recommendation 9

Require that Wardens document the specific reasons for denying an inmate's request for compassionate release.

Status: Resolved.

BOP Response: The BOP concurred with this recommendation, stating that the new electronic tracking system procedures will require Wardens to provide the reason for denying an inmate's compassionate release request.

OIG Analysis: The BOP's planned action is responsive to this recommendation. Please provide the OIG with a screenshot of the electronic tracking system that indicates how a Warden will document the specific reasons for denying an inmate's request for compassionate release.

Recommendation 10

Include as part of BOP program compliance reviews an element for reviewing compassionate release determinations made by Wardens.

Status: Resolved.

BOP Response: The BOP concurred with this recommendation, stating that compliance reviews involving compassionate release will affect several disciplines at the institution level and that it will review its program review policies to ensure guideline steps, by discipline, are incorporated into existing Program Review Guidelines.

OIG Analysis: The BOP's planned action is responsive to this recommendation. Please provide the OIG with copies of the revised Program Review Guidelines that ensure guideline steps, by discipline, involving compassionate release are included in institution compliance reviews.

Recommendation 11

Collect and assess the costs for providing health services to inmates diagnosed with terminal medical conditions and a limited life expectancy, and severely debilitating medical conditions.

Status: Resolved.

BOP Response: The BOP partially concurred with this recommendation, stating that it could be useful to track an estimated cost savings for inmates for whom the BOP submitted compassionate release motions to the sentencing judges and the judges granted early release. However, the BOP stated that it would be time and labor intensive to attempt to calculate medical costs for all inmates who have been diagnosed with terminal medical conditions and a limited life expectancy and non-terminal medical conditions. The BOP stated that these costs will likely vary in each individual case depending on the intensity of medical and custodial care needed over time, the unpredictable nature of an inmate's medical condition and costs of medical treatment over the course of care, and the area of the country in which the care is being provided, among other factors. The BOP also stated that any calculations would have to be based on estimates and average costs. Therefore, the BOP will use the current Actual Annual Cost of Incarceration Rate for each BOP Medical Referral Center and calculate the estimated cost avoidance related to each BOP-approved compassionate release case in which the inmate is ultimately released. The BOP requested that this recommendation be closed.

OIG Analysis: The BOP's planned action is partially responsive to this recommendation. The OIG agrees that it would be useful to track the estimated cost savings for inmates for whom the BOP submitted compassionate release motions to the sentencing judges and the judges granted early release. The OIG also agrees that costs will vary for each individual. However, the OIG believes the BOP is capable of identifying individual costs for inmates typically associated with compassionate release, including those inmates diagnosed with a terminal illness or severely debilitated condition. For example, the Health Services Administrator at one Medical Referral Center explained to the OIG that the institution-verified costs vary from patient to patient because the institution, using a spreadsheet, tracks the specific costs for each inmate, including inmates diagnosed with a specific medical condition, such as cancer.

The OIG believes the care for inmates associated with compassionate release is unique and must be identified individually to fully understand the per-inmate cost, as well as the savings realized by the release of these inmates. Therefore, the OIG encourages the BOP to coordinate with its Medical Referral Centers to better understand all efforts made to identify individual costs per inmate and how those efforts could be applied to the compassionate release program. Please provide the OIG with estimated cost savings using the current Actual Annual Cost of Incarceration Rate for each BOP Medical Referral Center for inmates approved and released for compassionate release for calendar years 2006 through 2011. In addition, please provide the OIG with a description of any efforts made by the BOP to coordinate with its Medical Referral Centers to better understand all efforts made to identify individual costs per inmate and how those efforts could be applied to the compassionate release program.

End Notes

[1] For inmates whose offenses occurred on or after November 1, 1987, the applicable statute is 18 U.S.C. § 3582(c)(1)(A). For inmates whose offenses occurred before November 1, 1987, 18 U.S.C. § 4205(g) remains the controlling law, even though it was repealed as part of the restructuring of federal sentencing law under the *Sentencing Reform Act.*

[2] In response to a working draft of this report, the BOP cited to the legislative history of 18 U.S.C. § 3582(c), which referenced terminal illness as an extraordinary and compelling circumstance in which a motion under this provision would be warranted. The BOP stated

that the legislative history helps to explain the approach the BOP has traditionally exercised in relation to compassionate release requests.

[3] BOP officials and institution staff use "compassionate release" and "reduction in sentence" interchangeably to refer to this program. In this report, we refer to the program as compassionate release.

[4] BOP institutions are not required to have handbooks, although we found that most institutions create their own handbooks.

[5] We recognize that, depending upon the nature of the medical condition and the financial and health insurance circumstances of the inmate, in at least some situations the inmate's release may result in additional health care costs to other government programs, such as Medicare or Medicaid.

[6] 18 U.S.C. § 3582(c)(1)(A), which applies to inmates whose offense occurred on or after November 1, 1987. For inmates whose offense occurred before that date, 18 U.S.C. § 4205(g) contains a similar provision and remains applicable to those inmates even though the statute was repealed as part of the *Sentencing Reform Act of 1984.* BOP officials and institution staff use "compassionate release" and "reduction in sentence" interchangeably to refer to this program. In this report, we refer to the program as compassionate release.

[7] The regulations are found at 28 C.F.R. § 571, subpart G, and apply to all inmates, regardless of the date of offense.

[8] There are currently 119 BOP-operated facilities. Our review is based on the 117 BOP facilities that were operational during the course of fieldwork.

[9] Average based on the number of inmates approved and released during the scope of our review, 2006 through 2011.

[10] BOP Program Statement 1330.16, Administrative Remedy Program, establishes formal procedures for an inmate to seek review of any issue related to their incarceration.

[11] On February 28, 2013, the BOP published an interim rule that expedited the compassionate release process by removing the Regional Director level of review, effective April 1, 2013. See Compassionate Release; Technical Changes, Interim Rule, 78 Fed. Reg. 40,13478 (Feb. 28, 2013).

[12] The BOP's Central Office is located in Washington, D.C. The following Central Office officials and their staff have roles in the compassionate release review process: the Director of BOP; Medical Director and Assistant Director of the Health Services Division; General Counsel and Assistant Director of the Office of General Counsel; and the Assistant Director of the Correctional Programs Division.

[13] The BOP's General Counsel told us that she reviews requests to determine if they are medically appropriate. If the appropriateness of a medical request is questionable, she meets with the Director to discuss the medical circumstances of the request.

[14] We were told that, while a denial letter may be signed by the General Counsel, all denials are in consultation and concurrence with the BOP Director.

[15] If the original sentence included a term of supervised release to follow the initially imposed term of imprisonment, the Warden must have included in the referral to the BOP Director confirmation that release plans were approved by the appropriate U.S. Probation Office. If the inmate will be released to an area outside the sentencing district, the U.S. Probation Office assuming supervision must be contacted. The role of the U.S. Probation Office was not part of this review because it is not a Department component.

[16] In 28 U.S.C. § 994(t), Congress directed the U.S. Sentencing Commission to promulgate general policy statements regarding the sentencing modification provisions in 18 U.S.C. § 3582(c)(1)(A) and to describe what should be considered extraordinary and compelling

reasons for sentence reduction, including the criteria to be applied and a list of specific examples. Rehabilitation of the defendant alone shall not be considered an extraordinary and compelling reason.

[17] U.S. Sentencing Guidelines, § 1B1.13: Reduction in Term of Imprisonment as a Result of Motion by Director of Bureau of Prisons (Policy Statement). U.S. Sentencing Guidelines, § 1B1.13, was enacted in 2006, with definitions iĞiv provided in 2007.

[18] A D.C. Code offender is a prisoner incarcerated in a BOP institution who was sentenced by the U.S. District Court for the District of Columbia or by the District of Columbia Superior Court after conviction for a D.C. Code offense.

[19] We also interviewed a second ODAG official who started in the ODAG in 2012. At the time of our fieldwork, this official had reviewed only one compassionate release request, in May 2012, which was outside the scope of our review.

[20] This institution's program supplement defines a terminal illness as "an illness which is progressive and will inevitably result in the patient's death regardless of treatment" and life expectancy as "a clinical attempt to quantify the time that a terminally ill patient has remaining to live."

[21] One institution's supplement contained "Procedures for Non-Medical Request for Reduction in Sentence" and stated that "Unit Management will determine if the request merits further recommendation," but did not provide the circumstances or criteria by which Unit Management should evaluate a non-medical request.

[22] In response to a working draft of this report, the BOP's Deputy General Counsel said that even with a consistent policy for evaluating compassionate release requests, there will still be some subjective determinations by the doctors. For example, a doctor could look at an inmate's medical history, response to treatment, or other factors and suggest a 1-year life expectancy, whereas another doctor could suggest a 2- or 3-year life expectancy. He added that doctors' opinions and patient conditions may vary from case to case. While the OIG recognizes that doctors' opinions and patient conditions vary and that accurately predicting life expectancy is difficult, we do not believe, as discussed below, that such difficulty justifies failing to provide BOP staff with any criteria for evaluating these requests.

[23] In response to a working draft of this report, the BOP also stated that establishing adequate release plans is a challenging task because of the level of medical care often needed for these seriously ill and often terminal inmates. The BOP is unable to recommend a compassionate release request if an adequate release plan is not in place. Therefore, subjective determinations and factors critical to whether an inmate should be released will likely limit the number of inmates who may otherwise be eligible for compassionate release.

[24] For those inmates requesting compassionate release for medical conditions other than cancer, the multi-disciplinary committee considers the opinion of the inmate's primary doctor.

[25] In response to our questionnaire, 99 of the 100 Wardens referenced multiple resources that they used when evaluating medical requests for compassionate release. Aside from the three Wardens who referenced the Clinical Guidelines, the Wardens reported using resources such as the Program Statement; input from institution, Regional Office, and Central Office staff; outside sources, such as the USAOs and U.S. Probation Offices; and inmate records, including medical records and court documents.

[26] In response to a working draft of this report, the BOP stated that it withdrew the first case from ODAG review after further consideration and that the second case was not forwarded to the ODAG because the BOP did not support the compassionate release request.

[27] We are concerned about such a lengthy potential delay in issuing a revised Program Statement given the lack of guidance in the existing Program Statement.

[28] On pages 40 to 41, we discuss the BOP's efforts to track the length of time to process requests.

[29] BOP Program Statement 1330.16, Administrative Remedy Program, effective August 6, 2002.

[30] The Program Statement permits a Warden or an Institution's Administrative Remedy Coordinator to waive the requirement of the informal resolution process "when the inmate demonstrates an acceptable reason for bypassing informal resolution."

[31] See pages 40 to 41 for our analysis of BOP administrative remedy data for inmate appeals to compassionate release decisions.

[32] BOP institutions are not required to have handbooks. However, most institutions create handbooks for their inmates and the contents vary, including whether and what information is included about the compassionate release program.

[33] 28 C.F.R. § 571.60-.64.

[34] BOP Program Statement 5290.14, Admission and Orientation (A&O) Program. The Program Statement requires that the A&O program at all BOP institutions include, at a minimum, all areas identified on the Institution Admission and Orientation Program Checklist. However, the compassionate release program is not on the checklist.

[35] We reviewed handbooks that were available on the BOP's website. Six institutions' handbooks were not available on the website.

[36] BOP Program Statement 5322.12, Inmate Classification and Program Review.

[37] We received 100 responses to our questionnaire from institution Wardens. However, in 11 of the 100 responses, Wardens did not rank the most common method used to inform inmates about the compassionate release program as requested by the OIG. Therefore, we did not include these 11 responses in our analysis of this question.

[38] We requested, and the BOP provided, the most current handbook for these institutions to verify that we reviewed the most current version.

[39] The BOP provided the OIG with 212 case files requesting compassionate release that the BOP's Office of General Counsel received from 2006 through 2011. However, one was a duplicate case file for an inmate's approved request. We reviewed 208 of those case files. We did not review the case files for three inmates because they had not received a decision from the BOP Director. In one of those cases, the inmate had her sentence vacated by the court, one withdrew his request, and one had his case referred for a "criminal matter."

[40] Two Wardens did not respond to this question.

[41] SENTRY is the BOP's primary mission support database. The system collects, maintains, and tracks critical inmate information, including inmate location, medical history, behavior history, and release data. Inmate deaths are also entered into SENTRY, but there is no code to determine if deceased inmates were awaiting compassionate release consideration.

[42] We confirmed that the remaining 12 inmates were not released pursuant to compassionate release.

[43] On March 15, 2012, the BOP's Chief of Sentence Computation sent an e-mail to the Designation and Sentence Computation Center staff reminding them that when they receive a sentence reduction that was completed based upon the BOP's authority under 18 U.S.C. § 3582(c)(1)(A), the "Basis for Change Code," "81-3582 BOP MOTION, or 82-3582 LOWERED SENTENCE RANGE - BUREAU OF PRISONS" should be used.

[44] The administrative remedy program allows an inmate to seek formal review of an issue relating to any aspect of his or her confinement.

[45] One non-medical request was denied by the Warden and Regional Director, as well as the National Inmate Appeals Administrator (Office of General Counsel) through the BOP's administrative remedy program. After the inmate filed a lawsuit against the BOP questioning the BOP's discretion to consider compassionate release requests, the Director

agreed to consider the inmate's request. The second non-medical request was approved by the Warden, but the Regional Director did not provide a recommendation to approve or deny. Rather, the Regional Director forwarded the request to the BOP's Central Office for consideration. The BOP Director denied both requests.

[46] We reviewed appeals filed by inmates under the BOP's administrative remedy program using a BP-10 form (for those requests denied by the Warden) or a BP-11 form (for those requests denied by the Regional Director) for 2006 through 2011. We did not request data on the BP-9 form (appeals to the Warden) because, in the case of compassionate release, procedures require that the Warden review the inmate's original request for compassionate release.

[47] We also found that one inmate died during consideration of the inmate's request by a Regional Director.

[48] An "Inmate Request to Staff Member" is a formal BOP document used by inmates to address written questions, requests, or concerns from any BOP employee. BOP staff commonly refers to this document as a "Cop-Out."

[49] The letter from the court stated that the court had received the inmate's request for compassionate release consideration and that the court had communicated with the several individuals at the BOP regarding the request. The BOP informed the court of the date the process of determining whether the inmate qualified for compassionate release would begin. The court wrote that the BOP "informed the court that the process involves multiple determinations and reviews, and therefore generally takes three to four months."

[50] The average time to process these requests does not include time taken for appeals through the BOP's administrative remedy program. As previously discussed, an inmate could wait up to 90 days for all levels of review to respond to an appeal prior to a final administrative decision, with additional time consumed by extensions to officials' deadlines for responses and by the inmate's efforts to prepare the submission for each level of the process.

[51] Of the 273 inmates who appealed an issue relating to his or her compassionate release request, 163 (60 percent) filed multiple appeals. For example, one inmate filed 12 appeals from 2010 through 2011 to both a Regional Director (6) and the General Counsel (6). All of this inmate's appeals were "Closed" or "Rejected" for a number of reasons, including that the inmate's appeal: (1) was not timely, (2) was repetitive of a previous filing, (3) did not include required paperwork, and (4) was submitted to the wrong level of review.

[52] Program Review Guidelines, Correctional Programs, Number G5000I.07 (June 3, 2011).

[53] We recognize that, depending upon the nature of the medical condition and the financial and health insurance circumstances of the inmate, in at least some situations the inmate's release may result in additional health care costs to other government programs, such as Medicare or Medicaid.

[54] The BOP's daily medical per capita rate is derived by taking total BOP Medical Obligations (all expenses charged to the Medical Program Area, including salaries and operational costs) incurred over a fiscal year divided by the average inmate population.

[55] The cost savings calculations are based on "Average Daily/Annual Per Capita Rates (with support costs)" provided by the BOP for FY 2007 through FY 2011; specifically, the annual cost of $57,962 for incarcerating an inmate at a BOP medical referral center in FY 2011.

[56] According to data from the Bureau of Justice Statistics (BJS), an average of 322 inmates died per year in BOP custody from 2001 to 2009 from an illness. U.S. Department of Justice, Office of Justice Programs, Bureau of Justice Statistics, *Prison and Jail Deaths in Custody, 2000–2009 – Statistical Tables,* NCJ236219 (December 2011). According to the BJS, with the exception of AIDS-related deaths, the BOP does not distinguish illness deaths by a specific cause of death, such as cancer or other diseases.

[57] U.S. Department of Justice, Federal Prison System, FY 2013 Performance Budget Congressional Submission, Salaries and Expenses.

[58] On March 6, 2012, as part of an initial data and information request, the OIG requested all documents related to the BOP's plan to expand the compassionate release program and the data and documentation supporting its FY 2013 Performance Budget Submission. During the course of our fieldwork, the BOP was unable to provide any documents related to its plan to expand the compassionate release program. On April 18, 2013, in response to our draft report and after the OIG had completed its review, the BOP provided one-page summaries of possible scenarios to expand the compassionate release program; pages from charts examining cost-savings options, including pages that describe possible expansion of the compassionate release program; and other working drafts of documents. While these documents provided more specific data, as well as additional context into possible scenarios to expand the compassionate release program, we found no documentation that supports that any scenario was actually implemented.

[59] U.S. Department of Justice, Office of the Inspector General, "Top Management and Performance Challenges in the Department of Justice – 2012," November 7, 2012.

[60] U.S. Government Accountability Office, *Bureau of Prisons: Growing Inmate Crowding Negatively Affects Inmates, Staff, and Infrastructure*, GAO-12-743 (September 2012).

[61] The BOP's Federal Medical Centers provide a range of medical and mental health services to inmates. The BOP does not track inmates with terminal illnesses or severely debilitating medical conditions. Therefore, neither the BOP nor the OIG can determine how many inmates incarcerated in BOP medical centers would be candidates for compassionate release consideration.

[62] We provided the FBI information on all 142 inmates released from 2006 through 2011. In 2011, one inmate was approved for release but died before actually being released. This inmate was not included in our recidivism analysis.

[63] One inmate was rearrested on three separate occasions after the compassionate release date. The first two arrests were within 3 years of the inmate's release date. The inmate's third arrest was just over 3 years after the release date.

[64] The Federal Bureau of Prisons, *Recidivism Among Federal Prisoners Released in 1987*, August 4, 1994.

[65] The inmate's sentence was later modified to 84 months of imprisonment, according to FBI data.

[66] The BOP provided the OIG with 212 cases files that the BOP OGC received from 2006 through 2011. We reviewed 208 case files where a decision to approve or deny was made, or the inmate died before a decision. We did not include one duplicate case file for an approved inmate. In addition, we did not review the case files for three inmates who did not receive a decision, including one inmate whose sentence was vacated by the court, one inmate who withdrew the request, and one inmate whose case was referred for a criminal matter.

In: The Federal Bureau of Prisons' … ISBN 978-1-62808-318-7
Editor: Josiah N. Marleins

Chapter 2

PRISON AND JAIL DEATHS IN CUSTODY, 2000-2009 - STATISTICAL TABLES*

Margaret E. Noonan and E. Ann Carson

This report provides an update to annual tables based on the Bureau of Justice Statistics' (BJS) Deaths in Custody Reporting Program (DCRP), a data collection that measures inmate mortality data in state prisons and local jails by the number and causes of deaths. In 2008, 960 inmates died in U.S. jails (a mortality rate of 123 deaths per 100,000 jail inmates). In 2009, 948 inmates died in U.S. jails (a rate of 127 deaths per 100,000 jail inmates). State prison facilities reported 3,452 inmate deaths in 2008 (a rate of 260 deaths per 100,000 prison inmates) and 3,408 inmate deaths in 2009 (257 deaths per 100,000 prison inmates). Consistent with data from previous years, local jail deaths constituted approximately 25% of inmate deaths in adult correctional facilities nationwide.

The number of inmate deaths in jails increased each year between 2000 and 2007 (from 904 to 1,102 inmate deaths), increasing 22% during this period. In 2008, the number of deaths in jails declined 13% to 960 inmate deaths, and decreased an additional 1% in 2009 to 948 deaths (**figure 1**). The decline in 2008 was the first decline in jail mortality data since BJS began collecting data annually for the DCRP in 2000.

From 2007 to 2008, 918 jails reported a change in the number of deaths to the DCRP. Among these jails, 324 reported a total increase of 452 deaths and

---

* These statistical tables, NCJ 236219, were released by the U.S. Department of Justice, Office of Justice Programs, Bureau of Justice Statistics, December 2011.

402 jails reported a total decrease of 594 deaths, for a net decrease of 142 deaths in 2008. The majority of jails reporting a decline (74%) registered one less death in 2008 than in 2007. Nine jails reported a total decrease of 69 deaths (12% of the total decline). All nine of these jails held at least 2,500 inmates on an average day in 2007 and 2008.

In general, the number of deaths in state prisons rose each year between 2001 and 2008 (from 2,877 to 3,452 inmate deaths), a 20% increase **(figure 2)**. In 2009, the number of deaths in prisons dropped to 3,408, a 1% decrease.

Statistical tables in this report detail prison and jail deaths in custody. The tables present mortality data by cause of death, selected decedent characteristics, and state.

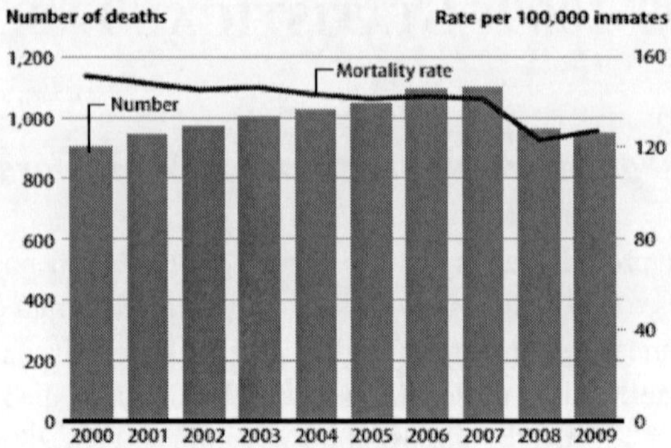

Figure 1. Jail inmate deaths in custody, 2000–2009.

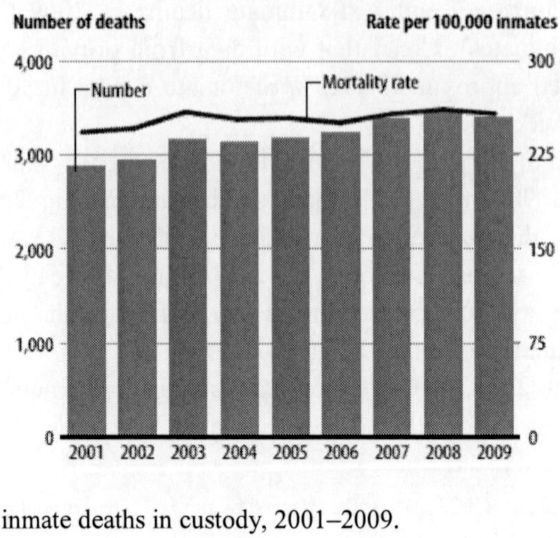

Figure 2. Prison inmate deaths in custody, 2001–2009.

SUMMARY FINDINGS: JAILS

Cause of Death

- After increasing an average of 3% annually between 2000 and 2007, the number of inmate deaths in jails declined 13% in 2008. In 2009, the number of jail deaths remained relatively stable (down 1% from 2008) **(table 1)**.
- Among the causes of inmate deaths in jails, AIDS-related deaths had the largest decline, decreasing by more than half (54%) between 2000 and 2009.
- Between 2000 and 2009, suicide (29%) and heart disease (22%) were the leading causes of deaths in jails, accounting for over half (51%) of all deaths in jails **(table 2)**.
- Death by drug or alcohol intoxication (7%) was the third leading single cause of death in jails between 2000 and 2009. No other single cause of death accounted for more than 5% of jail deaths during this period.
- Suicide rates in jails dropped every year between 2001 and 2007 (from 49 to 36 deaths per 100,000), before increasing in 2009 (41 deaths per 100,000) **(table 3)**.
- The jail mortality rate declined 13% between 2007 and 2008 (from 141 to 123 deaths per 100,000 jail inmates). The mortality rate increased in 2009 (127 deaths per 100,000), but this rate was still lower than the rate in 2007.

Decedent Characteristics

- Males constituted 88% of the jail population and 88% of jail deaths over the 10-year period. Females (132 deaths per 100,000) and males (141 deaths per 100,000) died at nearly equal rates between 2000 and 2009 (table 4).
- Whites (43% of the jail population) had a mortality rate in jails between 1.6 and 4.7 times that of any other race or ethnic group.
- American Indians and Alaska Natives accounted for about 2% of jail deaths, and Asians, Hawaiians, or other Pacific Islanders accounted for less than 1% of deaths in jails between 2000 and 2009 (table 5).

- Between 2000 and 2009, jail inmates age 55 or older were between 5 and 7 times more likely to die than inmates age 54 or younger. During this period, the annual mortality rate for jail inmates age 55 or older ranged from 666 to 870 deaths per 100,000 (table 6).

State-Level Jail Populations

- California, Texas, New York, and Florida reported 35% of all jail deaths. These states also had the largest jail populations and averaged 32% of the total jail average daily population reported to the DCRP between 2000 and 2009 (table 7).
- Between 2000 and 2009, nearly all (from 97% to 99%) of the approximately 2,800 jail jurisdictions in the U.S. submitted population and mortality data to the DCRP. These jurisdictions reported a total of 10,005 deaths over the ten-year period (table 9).

Cause of Death by Decedent Characteristics

- Males accounted for 98% of homicides in jails between 2000 and 2009 **(table 11)**.
- Between 2000 and 2009, males committed suicide (43 deaths per 100,000) at a higher rate than females (27 deaths per 100,000) in jails. Over this period, males were 1.6 times more likely to die by suicide than females, and females were 1.7 times more likely to die by intoxication than males **(table 12)**.
- Between 2000 and 2009, whites had the highest suicide rate in jail (80 deaths per 100,000). Hispanics/Latinos (25 deaths per 100,000) were 3 times less likely to commit suicide than whites in jails and 1.6 times more likely to commit suicide in jails than blacks/African Americans (16 deaths per 100,000).
- White, black/African American, and Hispanic/Latino inmates had equal homicide rates in jails (3 deaths per 100,000).
- In jails, the oldest inmates (age 55 or older) and the youngest inmates (age 17 or younger) had the highest suicide mortality rates (60 and 55 deaths per 100,000, respectively). Jail inmates age 55 or older were 3 times more likely than younger inmates to die of an accident.

SUMMARY FINDINGS: PRISONS

Cause of Death

- In general, the number of deaths in prisons increased each year between 2001 and 2008, increasing 20% during this period. Between 2008 and 2009, both the number of deaths and mortality rates remained relatively stable, declining 1% each **(table 13)**.
- Among the causes of inmate deaths in prisons, AIDS-related deaths had the largest decline (down 65%) between 2001 and 2009.
- Between 2001 and 2009, illness-related deaths accounted for 9 out of 10 prison deaths **(table 14)**.
- Heart disease (26%) and cancer (23%) were the leading single causes of illness-related deaths in prisons, together accounting for nearly half (49%) of all prison deaths between 2001 and 2009.
- Liver disease was the third leading single cause of death in prisons, accounting for 7% of all deaths.
- Deaths due to intoxication, homicide, or accident were the least common causes of deaths, with none accounting for more than 2% of deaths in prisons.

Decedent Characteristics

- On average, males constituted 96% of the prison population over the 9-year period and 93% of all prison deaths (table 17).
- Prison inmates age 55 or older accounted for 41% of prison deaths but comprised 5% of the total prison population for the 9-year period.
- Whites made up 37% of the prison population and 50% of deaths in prisons between 2001 and 2009. White mortality rates were between 1.4 and 1.8 times higher than other race or ethnic groups during the 9-year period.
- Between 2001 and 2009, males in prisons died at rate of 260 deaths per 100,000, while females died at a rate of 153 deaths per 100,000 (table 19).
- During the 9-year period of prison data collection, the annual mortality rates for inmates age 55 or older ranged between 2,007 and 2,500 deaths per 100,000.

State-Level Prison Populations

- All 50 (100%) state departments of corrections participated in the DCRP between 2001 and 2009 (table 20).
- California, Texas, Florida, and New York had the four largest correctional populations in the United States. They averaged 37% of the total prison population and reported 37% of deaths to the DCRP between 2001 and 2009.

Cause of Death by Decedent Characteristics

- Males accounted for more than 99% of prison homicides between 2001 and 2009 **(table 23)**.
- With the exception of deaths due to drug or alcohol intoxication, American Indians, Alaska Natives, Asians, Hawaiians, or other Pacific Islanders each accounted for less than 1% of all deaths in prisons between 2001 and 2009.
- American Indians and Alaska Natives accounted for 3.1% of all drug or alcohol intoxication deaths in state prisons between 2001 and 2009.
- Males were twice as likely (19 deaths per 100,000) as females (8 deaths per 100,000) to die from liver disease. Males were 1.5 times more likely to commit suicide than females in prison between 2001 and 2009 **(table 24)**.
- Blacks/African Americans accounted for 68% of AIDS-related deaths and died from AIDS at a rate (21 per 100,000) that was three times that of whites (7 per 100,000) and twice that of Hispanics/Latinos (10 per 100,000) between 2001 and 2009.
- Inmates age 55 or older had the highest mortality rates due to heart disease (664 deaths per 100,000), cancer (639 deaths per 100,000), and liver disease (113 deaths per 100,000) over the entire 9-year DCRP collection.
- Prison inmates age 55 or older had the highest homicide rate (8 deaths per 100,000), which was between 1.6 and 2.7 times higher than any other age group from 2001 to 2009.

List of Tables

Table 1. Number of local jail inmate deaths, by cause of death, 2000–2009

Cause of death	2000	2001	2002	2003	2004	2005	2006	2007	2008[a]	2009
All causes	904	944	972	1,004	1,024	1,049	1,098	1,102	960	948
Illness	516	488	508	514	533	504	609	609	446	488
Heart disease	198	216	221	241	227	203	250	232	177	200
AIDS-related	57	59	51	54	52	40	54	43	31	26
Cancer	31	25	39	35	29	37	39	42	25	47
Respiratory diseases	32	19	23	22	35	22	27	49	35	31
Liver disease	22	26	24	29	31	31	24	39	33	30
All other illnesses[b]	176	143	150	133	159	171	215	204	145	154
Suicide	289	314	314	296	299	286	278	285	230	303
Drug/alcohol intoxication	37	58	55	89	77	84	87	79	43	64
Accident	25	35	35	28	32	24	32	18	15	26
Homicide	17	19	18	15	24	22	36	20	17	23
Other/unknown	20	30	42	62	59	129	56	91	209	44

Note: Cause of death rankings may differ from previously published 2000–2007 estimates because cause of death was ranked on all deaths from 2000 to 2009, which resulted in small changes within some categories.

[a] In 2008, a high number of cases were missing cause of death information. These cases were classified as other/unknown. See *Methodology* for more information.

[b] Includes other specified (such as cerebrovascular disease, influenza, cirrhosis, and other non-leading natural causes of death) as well as unspecified illnesses. See *Methodology* for details on illness classifications.

Source: Bureau of Justice Statistics, Deaths in Custody Reporting Program (DCRP).

Table 2. Percent of local jail inmate deaths, by cause of death, 2000–2009

Cause of death	2000	2001	2002	2003	2004	2005	2006	2007	2008[a]	2009
All causes	100%	100%	100%	100%	100%	100%	100%	100%	100%	100%
Illness	57.1%	51.7%	52.3%	51.2%	52.1%	48.0%	55.5%	55.3%	46.5%	51.5%
Heart disease	21.9	22.9	22.7	24.0	22.2	19.4	22.8	21.1	18.4	21.1
AIDS-related	6.3	6.3	5.2	5.4	5.1	3.8	4.9	3.9	3.2	2.7
Cancer	3.4	2.6	4.0	3.5	2.8	3.5	3.6	3.8	2.6	5.0
Respiratory diseases	3.5	2.0	2.4	2.2	3.4	2.1	2.5	4.4	3.6	3.3
Liver disease	2.4	2.8	2.5	2.9	3.0	3.0	2.2	3.5	3.4	3.2
All other illnesses[b]	19.5	15.1	15.5	13.3	15.6	16.3	19.5	18.6	15.1	16.2
Suicide	32.0%	33.3%	32.3%	29.5%	29.2%	27.3%	25.3%	25.9%	24.0%	32.0%
Drug/alcohol intoxication	4.1%	6.1%	5.7%	8.9%	7.5%	8.0%	7.9%	7.5%	4.5%	6.8%
Accident	2.8%	3.7%	3.6%	2.8%	3.1%	2.3%	2.9%	1.6%	1.6%	2.7%

Cause of death	2000	2001	2002	2003	2004	2005	2006	2007	2008a	2009
Homicide	1.9%	2.0%	1.9%	1.5%	2.3%	2.1%	3.3%	1.8%	1.8%	2.4%
Other/unknown	2.2%	3.2%	4.3%	6.2%	5.8%	12.3%	5.1%	8.3%	21.8%	4.6%

Note: Cause of death rankings may differ from previously published 2000-2007 estimates because cause of death was ranked on all deaths from 2000 to 2009, which resulted in small changes within some categories.

[a] In 2008, a high number of cases were missing cause of death information. These cases were classified as other/unknown. See *Methodology* for more information.

[b] Includes other specified (such as cerebrovascular disease, influenza, cirrhosis, and other non-leading natural causes of death) as well as unspecified illnesses. See *Methodology* for details on illness classifications.

Source: Bureau of Justice Statistics, Deaths in Custody Reporting Program (DCRP).

Table 3. Mortality rate per 100,000 local jail inmates, by cause of death, 2000–2009

Cause of death	2000	2001	2002	2003	2004	2005	2006	2007	2008[a]	2009
All causes	151	148	145	146	143	141	142	141	123	127
Illness	86	76	76	75	74	68	79	78	57	66
Heart disease	33	34	33	35	32	27	32	30	23	27
AIDS-related	10	9	8	8	7	5	7	5	4	3
Cancer	5	4	6	5	4	5	5	5	3	6
Respiratory diseases	5	3	3	3	5	3	3	6	4	4
Liver disease	4	4	4	4	4	4	3	5	4	4
All other illnesses[b]	29	22	22	19	22	23	28	26	19	21
Suicide	48	49	47	43	42	39	36	36	30	41
Drug/alcohol intoxication	6	9	8	13	11	11	11	10	6	9
Accident	4	5	5	4	4	3	4	2	2	3
Homicide	3	3	3	2	3	3	5	3	2	3
Other/unknown	3	5	6	9	8	17	7	12	27	6

Note: Cause of death rankings may differ from previously published 2000-2007 estimates because cause of death was ranked on all deaths from 2000 to 2009, which resulted in small changes within some categories. Mortality rates are based on the average daily population (ADP). In 2000 and 2001, ADP was estimated by taking the average of January 1st and December 31st one-day inmate population counts.

[a] In 2008, a high number of cases were missing cause of death information. These cases were classified as other/unknown. See *Methodology* for more information.

[b] Includes other specified (such as cerebrovascular disease, influenza, cirrhosis, and other non-leading natural causes of death) as well as unspecified illnesses. See *Methodology* for details on illness classifications.

Source: Bureau of Justice Statistics, Deaths in Custody Reporting Program (DCRP).

Table 4. Number of local jail inmate deaths, by selected characteristics, 2000–2009

Characteristic	2000	2001	2002	2003	2004	2005	2006	2007	2008[a]	2009
Total	904	944	972	1,004	1,024	1,049	1,098	1,102	960	948
Sex										
Male	813	849	865	869	895	930	969	972	841	838
Female	91	91	107	133	129	119	129	130	119	110
Race/Hispanic origin[b]										
White	453	515	536	538	502	561	531	549	513	535
Black/African American	305	284	305	324	360	333	409	399	311	271
Hispanic/Latino	118	116	113	119	135	118	127	125	107	108
American Indian or Alaska Native	9	13	5	10	13	14	17	12	11	21
Asian	5	6	4	6	10	6	9	12	13	8
Hawaiian or other										
Pacific Islander	1	1	1	0	0	1	1	1	0	0
Two or more races	2	0	0	0	0	1	0	2	2	0
Age										
17 or younger	8	8	7	5	7	5	6	4	6	3
18–24	89	107	101	103	105	108	103	101	84	86
25–34	184	193	186	212	211	193	196	199	168	173
35–44	265	282	337	284	300	285	313	293	247	236
45–54	239	240	237	266	264	276	306	323	276	257
55 or older	115	111	102	128	134	171	169	182	178	193
Legal status										
Convicted[c]	258	254	245	256	227	231	238	247	200	246
Unconvicted[d]	628	683	719	740	788	802	850	851	755	690
Time served										
7 or fewer days	329	348	362	398	399	385	387	392	347	364
8–30	169	176	163	177	181	193	202	185	163	164
31–60	108	105	104	93	112	109	125	137	109	100
61–120	116	125	120	121	112	129	149	146	122	114
121–180	56	63	74	72	75	70	80	82	66	52
180 or more	119	113	135	126	128	128	126	154	130	146

Note: Detail may not sum to total due to missing data.

[a] In 2008, a high number of cases were missing cause of death information. These cases were classified as other/unknown. See *Methodology* for more information.

[b] Excludes persons of Hispanic/Latino origin unless specified.

[c] Includes inmates who returned on a probation or parole violation. Forms were modified in 2009 to identify inmates who were convicted, or returned on a probation or parole violation. As with previous years, these cases are counted as convicted. See *Methodology* for more information on changes to the survey.

[d] Includes inmates whose status was marked as other or was unspecified.

Source: Bureau of Justice Statistics, Deaths in Custody Reporting Program (DCRP).

Table 5. Percent of local jail inmate deaths, by selected characteristics, 2000–2009

Characteristic	2000	2001	2002	2003	2004	2005	2006	2007	2008[a]	2009
Total Sex	100%	100%	100%	100%	100%	100%	100%	100%	100%	100%
Male	89.9%	90.3%	89.0%	86.7%	87.4%	88.7%	88.3%	88.2%	87.6%	88.4%
Female	10.1	9.7	11.0	13.3	12.6	11.3	11.7	11.8	12.4	11.6
Race/Hispanic origin[b]										
White	50.7%	55.1%	55.6%	54.0%	49.2%	54.3%	48.5%	49.9%	53.6%	56.7%
Black/African American	34.2	30.4	31.6	32.5	35.3	32.2	37.4	36.3	32.5	28.7
Hispanic/Latino	13.2	12.4	11.7	11.9	13.2	11.4	11.6	11.4	11.2	11.5
American Indian or Alaska Native	1.0	1.4	0.5	1.0	1.3	1.4	1.6	1.1	1.1	2.2
Asian	0.6	0.6	0.4	0.6	1.0	0.6	0.8	1.1	1.4	0.8
Hawaiian or other										
Pacific Islander	0.1	0.1	0.1	0.0	0.0	0.1	0.1	0.1	0.0	0.0
Two or more races	0.2	0.0	0.0	0.0	0.0	0.1	0.0	0.2	0.2	0.0
Age										
17 or younger	0.9%	0.9%	0.7%	0.5%	0.7%	0.5%	0.5%	0.4%	0.6%	0.3%
18–24	9.9	11.4	10.4	10.3	10.3	10.4	9.4	9.2	8.8	9.1
25–34	20.4	20.5	19.2	21.2	20.7	18.6	17.9	18.1	17.5	18.2
35–44	29.4	30.0	34.7	28.5	29.4	27.5	28.6	26.6	25.8	24.9
45–54	26.6	25.5	24.4	26.7	25.9	26.6	28.0	29.3	28.8	27.1
55 or older	12.8	11.8	10.5	12.8	13.1	16.5	15.5	16.5	18.6	20.4
Legal status										
Convicted[c]	29.1%	27.1%	25.4%	25.7%	22.4%	22.4%	21.9%	22.5%	20.9%	26.3%
Unconvicted[d]	70.9	72.9	74.6	74.3	77.6	77.6	78.1	77.5	79.1	73.7
Time served										
7 or fewer days	36.7%	37.4%	37.8%	40.3%	39.3%	38.0%	36.2%	35.8%	37.0%	38.7%
8–30	18.8	18.9	17.0	17.9	18.0	19.0	18.9	16.9	17.4	17.4
31–60	12.0	11.3	10.9	9.4	11.1	10.7	11.7	12.5	11.6	10.6
61–120	12.9	13.4	12.5	12.3	11.1	12.7	13.9	13.3	13.0	12.1
121–180	6.2	6.8	7.7	7.3	7.4	6.9	7.5	7.5	7.0	5.5
180 or more	13.3	12.2	14.1	12.8	12.7	12.6	11.8	14.1	13.9	15.5

Note: Detail may not sum to total due to missing data.

[a] In 2008, a high number of cases were missing cause of death information. These cases were classified as other/unknown. See *Methodology* for more information.

[b] Excludes persons of Hispanic/Latino origin unless specified.

[c] Includes inmates who returned on a probation or parole violation. Forms were modified in 2009 to identify inmates who were convicted, or returned on a probation or parole violation. As with previous years, these cases are counted as convicted. See *Methodology* for more information on changes to the survey.

[d] Includes inmates whose status was marked as other or was unspecified.

Source: Bureau of Justice Statistics, Deaths in Custody Reporting Program (DCRP).

Table 6. Mortality rate per 100,000 local jail inmates, by selected characteristics, 2000–2009

Characteristic	2000	2001	2002	2003	2004	2005	2006	2007	2008[a]	2009
Total	151	148	145	146	143	141	142	141	123	127
Sex										
Male	153	150	146	143	143	144	144	143	124	128
Female	133	123	138	162	147	126	129	129	120	121
Race/Hispanic origin[b]										
White	211	225	224	218	196	213	194	198	188	205
Black/African American	128	111	114	118	126	123	145	140	111	101
Hispanic/Latino	107	98	92	94	102	87	90	87	67	71
American Indian or Alaska Native	112	152	56	108	136	141	164	114	105	210
Asian	88	99	63	92	147	85	123	161	176	113
Hawaiian or other Pacific Islander	88 !	82 !	79 !	0	0	71 !	68 !	67 !	0	0
Two or more races	11 !	0	0	0	0	2 !	0	5!	4!	0
Age										
17 or younger	122 !	114 !	95 !	69 !	96 !	68 !	82 !	58 !	86!	44 !
18–24	52	59	53	53	53	53	49	48	40	42
25–34	96	94	87	96	92	82	80	81	67	71
35–44	169	168	193	160	165	153	153	157	138	143
45–54	396	372	352	362	326	312	316	300	260	256
55 or older	870	785	691	785	737	853	762	729	666	708
Legal status										
Convicted[c]	98	96	92	94	80	82	81	83	41	53
Unconvicted[d]	187	182	180	178	183	174	177	175	261	250

Note: Detail may not sum to total due to missing data. Mortality rates are based on the average daily population (ADP). In 2000 and 2001, ADP was estimated by taking the average of January 1st and December 31 one-day inmate population counts. Inmate populations for sex and legal status are based on the *Annual Survey of Jails* (ASJ), from 2000 through 2009. Inmate populations for age and race/Hispanic origin are based on the *Survey of Inmates in Local Jails* (SILJ) from 2000 through 2002, and on the *National Inmate Survey* (NIS) and the *Annual Survey of Jails* (ASJ), from 2003 through 2009. See the *Methodology* for these tables for more information on estimates of age.

! Interpret with caution; too few cases to provide a reliable rate. See *Methodology* for more information.

[a] In 2008, a high number of cases were missing cause of death information. These cases were classified as other/unknown. See *Methodology* for more information.

[b] Excludes persons of Hispanic/Latino origin unless specified.

[c] Includes inmates who returned on a probation or parole violation. Forms were modified in 2009 to identify inmates who were convicted, or returned on a probation or parole violation. As with previous years, these cases are counted as convicted. See *Methodology* for more information on changes to the survey.

[d] Includes inmates whose status was marked as other or was unspecified.

Sources: Bureau of Justice Statistics, Deaths in Custody Reporting Program (DCRP), *Annual Survey of Jails* (ASJ), *National Inmate Survey* (NIS), and *Survey of Inmates in Local Jails* (SILJ).

Table 7. Number of jail deaths, by state and year, 2000–2009

State	2000	2001	2002	2003	2004	2005	2006	2007	2008	2009
All states	904	944	972	1,004	1,024	1,049	1,098	1,102	960	948
Alabama	24	27	22	15	23	23	35	22	19	20
Alaska...		...	...	...	...	...	...	...	...	...
Arizona	15	18	24	16	12	27	19	21	12	11
Arkansas	9	13	14	22	13	7	11	10	15	5
California	109	124	131	126	120	156	127	129	107	132
Colorado	13	16	14	13	11	18	13	21	21	14
Connecticut	...	...	...	...	...	...	...	...	...	...
Delaware	...	...	...	...	...	...	...	...	...	...
District of Columbia	4	0	10	12	13	11	12	10	7	8
Florida	82	100	79	85	86	79	99	103	77	87
Georgia	38	39	50	45	54	42	47	44	55	45
Hawaii...		...	...	...	...	...	...	...	...	...
Idaho	3	3	1	2	1	7	5	7	1	6
Illinois	31	21	22	30	41	25	37	31	28	29
Indiana	21	21	14	23	18	16	27	18	11	16
Iowa	2	4	3	1	4	4	3	5	2	6
Kansas	9	9	12	10	15	11	10	7	12	11
Kentucky	16	13	12	14	16	22	21	25	22	17
Louisiana	10	22	22	32	41	31	26	31	34	22
Maine	2	2	7	3	2	1	5	1	1	2
Maryland	22	20	20	25	15	23	27	32	25	20
Massachusetts	5	10	16	9	8	21	14	14	17	17
Michigan	23	17	18	26	20	29	21	18	12	20
Minnesota	6	8	6	9	9	8	11	8	4	3
Mississippi	9	12	17	18	17	16	18	18	14	13
Missouri	16	14	8	17	6	10	13	25	18	20
Montana	3	1	5	5	3	6	1	2	2	6
Nebraska	5	5	6	2	4	2	6	2	5	7
Nevada	15	18	6	6	8	14	9	10	8	14
New Hampshire	3	2	5	3	3	1	4	4	2	5
New Jersey	31	17	17	38	34	32	36	34	27	25
New Mexico	15	9	9	7	17	11	21	15	11	11
New York	57	52	51	47	43	51	52	52	32	35
North Carolina	15	17	32	22	21	18	21	28	19	21
North Dakota	1	1	2	2	1	0	2	1	1	2
Ohio	23	20	30	30	19	24	26	26	23	27
Oklahoma	15	18	9	13	14	18	21	24	17	17
Oregon	10	10	7	7	15	8	11	4	15	7
Pennsylvania	38	50	51	53	66	57	56	55	44	36
Rhode Island	...	...	...	...	...	...	...	...	...	...
South Carolina	17	23	17	11	16	19	21	14	19	15
South Dakota	4	2	1	0	1	3	1	1	2	2
Tennessee	29	28	29	23	39	36	30	35	37	34

Table 7. (Continued)

State	2000	2001	2002	2003	2004	2005	2006	2007	2008	2009
Texas	97	84	97	96	99	91	98	90	86	76
Utah	6	6	13	7	11	10	7	11	6	12
Vermont	...	...	...	...	...	...	...	...	...	...
Virginia	34	41	36	42	34	30	36	59	50	38
Washington	8	10	11	17	11	11	19	15	16	14
West Virginia	2	6	2	6	6	6	6	4	6	7
Wisconsin	7	11	12	11	10	11	11	15	17	11
Wyoming	0	0	2	3	4	3	2	1	1	2

Note: Jails are locally run jurisdictions under the authority of a sheriff, county government, or other local authority. Jail jurisdictions include counties (parishes in Louisiana) or municipal governments that administer one or more local jails. See *Methodology* for more information on the function of jails.

... Not available. Prisons and jails form one integrated system. See the prison tables for mortality data.

Source: Bureau of Justice Statistics, Deaths in Custody Reporting Program (DCRP).

Table 8. Mortality rate per 100,000 local jail inmates, by state, 2000–2009

State	2000	2001	2002	2003	2004	2005	2006	2007	2008	2009
All states	151	148	145	146	143	141	142	141	123	127
Alabama	185	228	164	119	171	157	235	139	118	145
Alaska	...	...	...	...	...	...	...	...	...	...
Arizona	138	132	189	116	82	176	126	127	67	73!
Arkansas	171!	233	229	352	211	116!	172!	143!	203	67!
California	150	171	173	165	154	190	155	155	128	166
Colorado	142	154	126	111	95!	136	94	155	160	106
Connecticut	...	...	...	...	...	...	...	...	...	...
Delaware	...	...	...	...	...	...	...	...	...	...
District of Columbia	242!	0	316!	529	374	475!	346	318!	234!	259!
Florida	166	200	145	159	143	125	153	154	115	141
Georgia	113	110	132	114	128	94	103	98	115	97
Hawaii	...	...	...	...	...	...	...	...	...	...
Idaho	112!	101!	30!	59!	34!	178!	127!	172!	25!	160!
Illinois	178	107	106	140	201	84	181	150	134	148
Indiana	165	124	95	149	109	92	144	104	62	87
Iowa	66!	129!	83!	26!	110!	96!	75!	120!	49!	154!
Kansas	177!	159!	195	134!	219	148!	130!	95!	156	157!
Kentucky	139	68	86	97	98	134	124	138	122	95
Louisiana	44!	82	81	115	143	104	100	104	117	77
Maine	154!	142!	464!	191!	135!	64!	283!	61!	63!	127!
Maryland	210	182	166	199	116	181	207	228	184	164
Massachusetts	53!	91!	136	73!	61!	168	101	103	128	129

State	2000	2001	2002	2003	2004	2005	2006	2007	2008	2009
Michigan	145	103	108	156	111	159	112	98	68	118
Minnesota	121!	141!	101!	140!	128!	110!	151!	106!	56!	45!
Mississippi	91!	129	167	166	162	146	164	152	127	134
Missouri	211	171	89!	181	60!	97!	116	235	154	173
Montana	232!	53!	277!	260!	149!	288!	50!	116!	112!	344!
Nebraska	234!	211!	241!	80!	140!	68!	219!	68!	159!	204!
Nevada	288	333	106!	80!	116!	228	139!	131!	106!	181
New Hampshire	338!	145!	323!	192!	181!	54!	195!	196!	99!	237!
New Jersey	205	108	104	225	196	177	189	185	151	152
New Mexico	253	140!	136!	95!	210	128!	233	171	121!	133!
New York	208	181	166	154	141	166	161	166	106	124
North Carolina	122	132	212	144	128	100	115	147	98	128
North Dakota	162!	154!	268!	242!	114!	0	208!	113!	104!	223!
Ohio	143	118	161	153	96	122	126	127	119	135
Oklahoma	208	249	119!	158	154	179	191	222	169	162
Oregon	150!	132!	110!	106!	230	117!	165!	48!	238	117!
Pennsylvania	135	165	153	164	200	166	155	144	118	95
Rhode Island	...	...	...	...	...	...	...	...	...	...
South Carolina	194	218	140	100!	138	157	165	103	139	119
South Dakota	344!	176!	77!	0	66!	192!	61!	65!	141!	123!
Tennessee	143	138	138	100	168	149	92	139	139	129
Texas	167	154	173	159	157	169	144	130	124	113
Utah	112!	107!	223	112!	169!	156!	107!	160!	87!	173
Vermont	...	...	...	...	...	...	...	...	...	...
Virginia	170	185	152	168	133	113	127	200	173	134
Washington	93!	81!	91!	144	93!	85!	142	109	119	107
West Virginia	71!	185!	65!	182!	166!	147!	139!	92!	138!	171!
Wisconsin	54!	86!	89!	78!	69!	74!	73!	96	110	90!
Wyoming	0	0	163!	224!	267!	196!	131!	64!	59!	123!

Note: Jails are locally run jurisdictions under the authority of a sheriff, county government, or other local authority. Jail jurisdictions include counties (parishes in Louisiana) or municipal governments that administer one or more local jails. See *Methodology* for more information on the function of jails. Mortality rates are based on the average daily population (ADP). In 2000 and 2001, ADP was estimated by taking the average of January 1st and December 31 one-day inmate population counts. Mortality rates between states are not directly comparable because rates are not adjusted for age, sex, race, geographic location, or any other characteristic.

... Not available. Prisons and jails form one integrated system. See the prison tables for mortality data.

! Interpret with caution; estimate based on too few cases to provide a reliable rate. See *Methodology* for more information.

Source: Bureau of Justice Statistics, Deaths in Custody Reporting Program (DCRP).

Table 9. Number of jail jurisidictions reporting to the Deaths in Custody Reporting Program, by state and year, 2000–2009

State	2000	2001	2002	2003	2004	2005	2006	2007	2008	2009
All states	2,979	2,964	2,944	2,929	2,913	2,886	2,856	2,835	2,820	2,743
Alabama	152	150	148	147	146	143	137	133	126	116
Alaska...		...	...	...	...	...	...	...	...	...
Arizona	16	15	15	15	15	15	15	15	15	15
Arkansas	85	84	84	83	82	83	81	81	81	77
California	74	71	71	71	71	70	69	68	67	65
Colorado	57	57	57	57	57	57	55	55	55	55
Connecticut	...	...	...	...	...	...	...	...	...	...
Delaware	...	...	...	...	...	...	...	...	...	...
District of Columbia	1	1	1	1	1	1	1	1	1	1
Florida	69	69	69	69	68	68	68	68	68	66
Georgia	200	196	196	194	194	189	186	184	181	174
Hawaii...		...	...	...	...	...	...	...	...	...
Idaho	39	38	38	38	38	38	38	37	37	36
Illinois	91	90	91	91	90	91	90	90	90	90
Indiana	92	93	92	92	92	91	91	91	91	90
Iowa	94	93	93	93	93	93	93	93	93	92
Kansas	96	96	96	96	96	96	95	95	94	91
Kentucky	80	78	80	79	79	76	74	74	74	70
Louisiana	90	89	89	90	89	87	88	87	87	81
Maine	15	15	15	15	15	15	15	14	14	14
Maryland	25	25	25	25	25	25	25	25	25	24
Massachusetts	13	15	15	15	15	16	16	16	16	16
Michigan	83	83	82	82	82	82	81	81	81	81
Minnesota	76	76	76	76	76	77	76	76	75	73
Mississippi	92	91	92	90	89	86	84	85	84	80
Missouri	125	125	125	124	120	120	122	121	121	114
Montana	41	41	40	40	41	40	40	40	40	38
Nebraska	64	63	63	63	63	63	62	62	62	61
Nevada	20	20	20	20	20	20	20	20	20	20
New Hampshire	10	10	10	10	10	10	10	10	10	10
New Jersey	21	21	21	21	21	21	21	21	21	20
New Mexico	34	35	35	34	34	32	32	32	32	29
New York	60	60	60	60	60	60	60	59	59	57
North Carolina	96	96	96	96	95	95	95	95	94	89
North Dakota	23	23	23	23	23	23	22	21	21	22
Ohio	103	101	99	96	96	96	94	93	93	93
Oklahoma	100	100	100	99	98	96	94	93	93	88
Oregon	34	34	34	34	34	33	33	33	33	33
Pennsylvania	67	67	67	66	66	66	66	66	66	64
Rhode Island	...	...	...	...	...	...	...	...	...	...
South Carolina	51	50	51	50	50	50	50	50	50	49
South Dakota	28	29	29	29	29	28	28	28	28	26

State	2000	2001	2002	2003	2004	2005	2006	2007	2008	2009
Tennessee	103	103	102	102	102	102	101	100	100	95
Texas	253	252	249	249	246	246	246	241	240	236
Utah	26	26	26	26	26	26	26	26	26	26
Vermont	...	...	...	...	...	...	...	...	...	...
Virginia	76	75	75	75	75	73	69	67	67	67
Washington	60	60	59	58	58	57	57	57	57	57
West Virginia[a]	29	28	19	18	16	13	12	12	12	12
Wisconsin	71	71	71	71	71	71	71	71	71	69
Wyoming	22	22	22	22	22	22	22	22	22	22

Note: Reporting jails include all jails that reported population or death data to the Deaths in Custody Reporting Program (DCRP). All jails are asked to report population data regardless of whether an inmate death occurred. Jails are locally run jurisdictions under the authority of a sheriff, county government, or other local authority. Jail jurisdictions include counties (parishes in Louisiana) or municipal governments that administer one or more local jails. See *Methodology* for more information on the function of jails.

... Not available. Prisons and jails form one integrated system. See the prison tables for mortality data.

[a] In 2007, the Bureau of Justice Statistics began receiving data from a centralized regional jail respondent that covered all West Virginia jails.

Source: Bureau of Justice Statistics, Deaths in Custody Reporting Program (DCRP).

Table 10. Number of local jail inmate deaths, by cause of death and selected characteristics, 2000–2009

	Illness										
Characteristic	Heart disease	AIDS- related	Cancer	Respiratory diseases	Liver disease	All other illnesses[a]	Suicide	Drug/alcohol intoxication	Accident	Homicide	Other/unknown[b]
Total	2,165	467	349	295	289	1,650	2,894	673	270	211	742
Sex											
Male	1,948	407	314	240	271	1,368	2,661	543	244	207	638
Female	217	60	35	55	18	281	232	130	26	4	100
Race/Hispanic origin[c]											
White	1,002	77	147	130	159	677	2,022	407	171	77	364
Black/African American	920	330	159	126	62	707	421	159	65	94	258
Hispanic/Latino	193	57	35	32	61	227	337	90	26	37	91
American Indian or Alaska Native	21	1	2	5	5	13	59	11	3	0	5
Asian	10	2	5	0	0	14	38	1	4	1	4

Table 10. (Continued)

Characteristic	Illness: Heart disease	AIDS- related	Cancer	Respiratory diseases	Liver disease	All other illnesses[a]	Suicide	Drug/alcohol intoxication	Accident	Homicide	Other/unknown[b]
Hawaiian or other Pacific Islander	4	0	0	0	0	0	1	1	0	0	0
Two or more races	2	0	0	0	0	0	4	0	0	0	1
Age											
17 or younger	2	3	0	2	0	3	39	4	1	1	4
18–24	56	9	6	8	3	86	576	89	34	47	73
25–34	210	84	24	38	13	219	867	210	67	51	132
35–44	561	193	55	78	66	472	873	207	79	53	205
45–54	763	146	125	95	150	558	414	135	65	40	193
55 or older	569	31	139	74	57	310	118	26	24	18	117
Legal status											
Convicted[d]	655	126	99	76	77	439	508	115	79	52	176
Unconvicted[e]	1,492	336	248	214	212	1,199	2,370	554	190	153	538
Time served											
7 or fewer days	695	35	14	60	67	501	1,376	476	136	57	294
8–30	435	91	44	85	51	346	456	45	37	48	135
31–60	275	63	45	33	46	211	300	20	17	23	69
61–120	287	104	65	45	46	218	303	42	25	32	87
121–180	151	73	49	24	27	133	146	19	13	15	40
180 or more	281	98	126	42	51	214	282	55	38	33	85

Note: Detail may not sum to total due to missing data. Cause of death rankings may differ from previously published 2000-2007 estimates because cause of death was ranked on all deaths from 2000 to 2009, which resulted in small changes within some categories.

[a] Includes other specified (such as cerebrovascular disease, influenza, cirrhosis, and other non-leading natural causes of death) as well as unspecified illnesses. See *Methodology* for details on illness classifications.

[b] In 2008, a high number of cases were missing cause of death information. These cases were classified as other/unknown.

[c] Excludes persons of Hispanic/Latino origin unless specified.

[d] Includes inmates who returned on a probation or parole violation. Forms were modified in 2009 to identify inmates who were convicted, or returned on a probation or parole violation. As with previous years, these cases are counted as convicted. See *Methodology* for more information on changes to the survey.

[e] Includes inmates whose status was marked as other or was unspecified.

Source: Bureau of Justice Statistics, Deaths in Custody Reporting Program (DCRP).

Table 11. Percent of local jail inmate deaths, by cause of death and selected characteristics, 2000–2009

	Illness									
Characteristic	Heart disease	AIDS- related	Cancer	Respiratory diseases	Liver disease	All other illnessesa	Suicide	Drug/alcohol intoxication	Accident	Homicide
Total Sex	100%	100%	100%	100%	100%	100%	100%	100%	100%	100%
Male	90.0%	87.2%	90.0%	81.4%	93.8%	82.9%	91.9%	80.7%	90.4%	98.1%
Female	10.0	12.8	10.0	18.6	6.2	17.0	8.0	19.3	9.6	1.9
Race/Hispanic originb										
White	46.3%	16.5%	42.1%	44.1%	55.0%	41.0%	69.9%	60.5%	63.3%	36.5%
Black/African										
American	42.5	70.7	45.6	42.7	21.5	42.8	14.5	23.6	24.1	44.5
Hispanic/Latino	8.9	12.2	10.0	10.8	21.1	13.8	11.6	13.4	9.6	17.5
American Indian or Alaska Native	1.0	0.2	0.6	1.7	1.7	0.8	2.0	1.6	1.1	0.0
Asian	0.5	0.4	1.4	0.0	0.0	0.8	1.3	0.1	1.5	0.5
Hawaiian or other										
Pacific Islander	0.2	0.0	0.0	0.0	0.0	0.0	0.0	0.1	0.0	0.0
Two or more races	0.1	0.0	0.0	0.0	0.0	0.0	0.1	0.0	0.0	0.0
Age 17 or younger	0.1%	0.6%	0.0%	0.7%	0.0%	0.2%	1.3%	0.6%	0.4%	0.5%
18–24	2.6	1.9	1.7	2.7	1.0	5.2	19.9	13.2	12.6	22.3
25–34	9.7	18.0	6.9	12.9	4.5	13.3	30.0	31.2	24.8	24.2
35–44	25.9	41.3	15.8	26.4	22.8	28.6	30.2	30.8	29.3	25.1
45–54	35.2	31.3	35.8	32.2	51.9	33.8	14.3	20.1	24.1	19.0
55 or older	26.3	6.6	39.8	25.1	19.7	18.8	4.1	3.9	8.9	8.5
Legal status										
Convictedc	30.3%	27.0%	28.4%	25.8%	26.6%	26.6%	17.6%	17.1%	29.3%	24.6%
Unconvictedd	68.9	71.9	71.1	72.5	73.4	72.7	81.9	82.3	70.4	72.5
Time served 7 or fewer days	32.1%	7.5%	4.0%	20.3%	23.2%	30.4%	47.5%	70.7%	50.4%	27.0%
8–30	20.1	19.5	12.6	28.8	17.6	21.0	15.8	6.7	13.7	22.7
31–60	12.7	13.5	12.9	11.2	15.9	12.8	10.4	3.0	6.3	10.9
61–120	13.3	22.3	18.6	15.3	15.9	13.2	10.5	6.2	9.3	15.2
121–180	7.0	15.6	14.0	8.1	9.3	8.1	5.0	2.8	4.8	7.1
180 or more	13.0	21.0	36.1	14.2	17.6	13.0	9.7	8.2	14.1	15.6

Note: Detail may not sum to total due to missing data. Cause of death rankings may differ from previously published 2000-2007 estimates because cause of death was ranked on all deaths from 2000 to 2009, which resulted in small changes within some categories.

[a] Includes other specified (such as cerebrovascular disease, influenza, cirrhosis, and other non-leading natural causes of death) as well as unspecified illnesses. See *Methodology* for details on illness.

[b] Excludes persons of Hispanic/Latino origin unless specified.

[c] Includes inmates who returned on a probation or parole violation. Forms were modified in 2009 to identify inmates who were convicted, or returned on a probation or parole violation. As with previous years, these cases are counted as convicted. See *Methodology* for more information on changes to the survey.

[d] Includes inmates whose status was marked as other or was unspecified.

Source: Bureau of Justice Statistics, Deaths in Custody Reporting Program (DCRP).

Table 12. Average annual mortality rate per 100,000 local jail inmates, by cause of death and selected characteristics, 2000–2009

	Illness									
Characteristic	Heart disease	AIDS- related	Cancer	Respiratory diseases	Liver disease	All other illnesses[a]	Suicide	Drug/alcohol intoxication	Accident	Homicide
Total	30	7	5	4	4	23	41	9	4	3
Sex										
Male	31	7	5	4	4	22	43	9	4	3
Female	25	7	4	6	2	32	27	15	3	--!
Race/Hispanic origin[b]										
White	40	3	6	5	6	27	80	16	7	3
Black/African American	34	12	6	5	2	26	16	6	2	3
Hispanic/Latino	14	4	3	2	5	17	25	7	2	3
American Indian or Alaska Native	22	1!	2	5	5	14	62	12!	3	0
Asian	15!	3!	7	0	0	21	56	1!	6	1!
Hawaiian or other Pacific Islander	30!	0	0	0	0	0	7!	7!	0	0
Two or more races	1!	0	0	0	0	0	1!	0	0	0
Age										
17 or younger	3!	4!	0	3!	0	4!	55	6!	1!	1!
18–24	3	--!	--!	--!	--!	4	29	5	2	2
25–34	9	4	1	2	1	10	38	9	3	2
35–44	32	11	3	4	4	27	49	12	4	3
45–54	90	17	15	11	18	66	49	16	8	5
55 or older	288	16	70	37	29	157	60	13	12	9
Legal status										
Convicted[c]	21	4	3	2	2	14	16	4	2	2
Unconvicted[d]	38	9	6	5	5	30	60	14	5	4

Note: Detail may not sum to total due to missing data. Cause of death rankings may differ from previously published 2000-2007 estimates because cause of death was ranked on all deaths from 2000 to 2009, which resulted in small changes within some categories. Mortality rates are based on the average daily population (ADP). In 2000 and 2001,

ADP was estimated by taking the average of January 1st and December 31st one-day inmate population counts. Inmate populations for sex and legal status are based on the *Annual Survey of Jails* (ASJ), from 2000 through 2009. Inmate populations for age and race/Hispanic origin are based on the *Survey of Inmates in Local Jails* (SILJ) from 2000 through 2002, and on the *National Inmate Survey* (NIS) and the *Annual Survey of Jails* (ASJ), from 2003 through 2009. See *Methodology* for more information on age estimates.

-- Less than 0.5.

! Interpret with caution; too few cases to provide a reliable rate. See *Methodology* for more information.

[a] Includes other specified (such as cerebrovascular disease, influenza, cirrhosis, and other non-leading natural causes of death) as well as unspecified illnesses. See *Methodology* for details on illness classifications.

[b] Excludes persons of Hispanic/Latino origin unless specified.

[c] Includes inmates who returned on a probation or parole violation. Forms were modified in 2009 to identify inmates who were convicted, or returned on a probation or parole violation. As with previous years, these cases are counted as convicted. See *Methodology* for more information on changes to the survey.

[d] Includes inmates whose status was marked as other or was unspecified.

Sources: Bureau of Justice Statistics, Deaths in Custody Reporting Program (DCRP), *Annual Survey of Jails* (ASJ), *National Inmate Survey* (NIS), and *Survey of Inmates in Local Jails* (SILJ).

Table 13. Number of state prisoner deaths, by cause of death, 2001–2009

Cause of death	2001	2002	2003	2004	2005	2006	2007[a]	2008	2009
All causes	2,877	2,942	3,165	3,129	3,172	3,239	3,392	3,452	3,408
Illness	2,573	2,621	2,843	2,787	2,819	2,833	2,981	3,030	3,014
Heart disease	749	804	821	838	851	866	710	859	870
Cancer	628	650	776	710	763	765	600	858	911
Liver disease	225	201	248	219	237	244	190	234	258
AIDS-related	272	242	210	146	154	132	120	98	94
All other illnesses[b]	699	724	788	874	814	826	1,361	981	881
Suicide	169	168	199	200	213	220	216	197	201
Homicide	39	48	49	49	56	55	57	40	55
Drug/alcohol intoxication	35	37	23	22	37	57	41	58	50
Accident	23	31	26	34	30	33	29	26	31
Other/unknown	38	37	25	37	17	41	68	101	57

Note: Data may have been revised from previously published statistics to reflect updated information. Executions are not included; for data on executions, see *Capital Punishment, 2009 - Statistical Tables*.

[a] In 2007, a high number of cases were missing cause of death information. These cases were classified as all other illnesses.

[b] Includes other specified (such as cerebrovascular disease, influenza, cirrhosis, and other non-leading natural causes of death) as well as unspecified illnesses. See *Methodology* for details on illness classifications.

Source: Bureau of Justice Statistics, Deaths in Custody Reporting Program (DCRP).

Table 14. Percent of state prisoner deaths, by cause of death, 2001–2009

Cause of death	2001	2002	2003	2004	2005	2006	2007[a]	2008	2009
All causes	100%	100%	100%	100%	100%	100%	100%	100%	100%
Illness	89.4%	89.1%	89.8%	89.1%	88.9%	87.5%	87.9%	87.8%	88.4%
Heart disease	26.0	27.3	25.9	26.8	26.8	26.7	20.9	24.9	25.5
Cancer	21.8	22.1	24.5	22.7	24.1	23.6	17.7	24.9	26.7
Liver disease	7.8	6.8	7.8	7.0	7.5	7.5	5.6	6.8	7.6
AIDS-related	9.5	8.2	6.6	4.7	4.9	4.1	3.5	2.8	2.8
All other illnesses[b]	24.3	24.6	24.9	27.9	25.7	25.5	40.1	28.4	25.9
Suicide	5.9%	5.7%	6.3%	6.4%	6.7%	6.8%	6.4%	5.7%	5.9%
Homicide	1.4	1.6	1.5	1.6	1.8	1.7	1.7	1.2	1.6
Drug/alcohol intoxication	1.2	1.3	0.7	0.7	1.2	1.8	1.2	1.7	1.5
Accident	0.8	1.1	0.8	1.1	0.9	1.0	0.9	0.8	0.9
Other/unknown	1.3	1.3	0.8	1.2	0.5	1.3	2.0	2.9	1.7

Note: Data may have been revised from previously published statistics to reflect updated information. Executions are not included; for data on executions, see *Capital Punishment, 2009 - Statistical Tables.*

[a] In 2007, a high number of cases were missing cause of death information. These cases were classified as all other illnesses.

[b] Includes other specified (such as cerebrovascular disease, influenza, cirrhosis, and other non-leading natural causes of death) as well as unspecified illnesses. See *Methodology* for details on illness classifications.

Source: Bureau of Justice Statistics, Deaths in Custody Reporting Program (DCRP).

Table 15. Mortality rate per 100,000 state prisoners, by cause of death, 2001–2009

Cause of death	2001	2002	2003	2004	2005	2006	2007[a]	2008	2009
All causes	242	245	258	252	253	250	257	260	257
Illness	217	218	232	225	225	218	226	228	227
Heart disease	63	67	67	68	68	67	54	65	66
Cancer	53	54	63	57	61	59	46	65	69
Liver disease	19	17	20	18	19	19	14	18	19
AIDS-related	23	20	17	12	12	10	9	7	7
All other illnesses[b]	59	60	64	71	65	64	103	74	66
Suicide	14	14	16	16	17	17	16	15	15
Homicide	3	4	4	4	4	4	4	3	4
Drug/alcohol intoxication	3	3	2	2	3	4	3	4	4
Accident	2	3	2	3	2	3	2	2	2
Other/unknown	3	3	2	3	1	3	5	8	4

Note: Data are from the *Prisoners at Midyear* series. Data may have been revised from previously published statistics to reflect updated information. State prison mortality rates are per 100,000 inmates held in state custody (including private facilities) on June 30th of each year. The mortality rates presented are not adjusted for age, sex, race, geographic location, or any other characteristic. Executions are not included; for data on executions, see *Capital Punishment, 2009 - Statistical Tables.*

[a] In 2007, a high number of cases were missing cause of death information. These cases were classified as all other illnesses.

[b] Includes other specified (such as cerebrovascular disease, influenza, cirrhosis, and other non-leading natural causes of death) as well as unspecified illnesses. See *Methodology* for details on illness classifications.

Sources: Bureau of Justice Statistics, Deaths in Custody Reporting Program (DCRP), *National Prisoner Statistics* (NPS).

Table 16. Number of state prisoner deaths, by selected characteristics, 2001–2009

Characteristic	2001	2002	2003	2004	2005	2006	2007	2008	2009
Total	2,877	2,942	3,165	3,129	3,172	3,239	3,392	3,452	3,408
Sex									
Male	2,777	2,823	3,037	2,993	3,029	3,109	3,255	3,289	3,258
Female	100	119	126	136	143	130	137	163	150
Race/Hispanic origin[a]									
White	1,343	1,404	1,596	1,549	1,625	1,630	1,719	1,823	1,768
Black/African American	1,164	1,156	1,204	1,182	1,164	1,151	1,226	1,157	1,196
Hispanic/Latino	324	332	311	332	324	404	384	399	372
American Indian or									
Alaska Native	25	20	24	29	32	25	34	36	31
Asian	4	12	8	15	12	8	11	18	20
Hawaiian or other									
Pacific Islander	7	7	7	5	6	2	7	4	4
Other[b]	5	5	6	16	4	15	2	15	3
Age									
17 or younger	2	1	3	1	1	1	1	3	0
18–24	86	63	57	82	78	60	69	67	69
25–34	258	249	277	256	245	251	226	222	210
35–44	657	663	669	620	601	562	515	469	468
45–54	897	909	983	964	1,009	1,062	1,031	1,063	1,036
55 or older	972	1,055	1,171	1,204	1,237	1,302	1,550	1,628	1,624

Note: Detail may not sum to total due to missing data. Data may have been revised from previously published statistics to reflect updated information. Executions are not included; for data on executions, see *Capital Punishment, 2009 - Statistical Tables*.

[a] Excludes persons of Hispanic/Latino origin unless specified. bIncludes persons of two or more races or unknown race.

Source: Bureau of Justice Statistics, Deaths in Custody Reporting Program (DCRP).

Table 17. Percent of state prisoner deaths, by selected characteristics, 2001–2009

Characteristic	2001	2002	2003	2004	2005	2006	2007	2008	2009
Total Sex	100%	100%	100%	100%	100%	100%	100%	100%	100%
Male	96.5%	96.0%	96.0%	95.7%	95.5%	96.0%	96.0%	95.3%	95.6%
Female	3.5	4.0	4.0	4.3	4.5	4.0	4.0	4.7	4.4
Race/Hispanic origin[a]									
White	46.7%	47.7%	50.5%	49.5%	51.2%	50.3%	50.7%	52.8%	51.9%
Black/African American	40.5	39.3	38.0	37.8	36.7	35.5	36.1	33.5	35.1
Hispanic/Latino	11.3	11.3	9.8	10.6	10.2	12.5	11.3	11.6	10.9
American Indian or									
Alaska Native	0.9	0.7	0.8	0.9	1.0	0.8	1.0	1.0	0.9
Asian	0.1	0.4	0.2	0.5	0.4	0.3	0.3	0.5	0.6
Hawaiian or other									
Pacific Islander	0.2	0.2	0.2	0.2	0.2	0.1	0.2	0.1	0.1
Other[b]	0.2	0.2	0.2	0.5	0.1	0.5	0.1	0.4	0.1
Age									
17 or younger	0.1%	0.0%	0.1%	0.0%	0.0%	0.0%	0.0%	0.1%	0.0%
18–24	3.0	2.1	1.8	2.6	2.5	1.9	2.0	1.9	2.0
25–34	9.0	8.5	8.8	8.2	7.7	7.7	6.7	6.4	6.2
35–44	22.8	22.5	21.1	19.8	18.9	17.4	15.2	13.6	13.7
45–54	31.2	30.9	31.1	30.8	31.8	32.8	30.4	30.8	30.4
55 or older	33.8	35.9	37.0	38.5	39.0	40.2	45.7	47.2	47.7

Note: Detail may not sum to total due to missing data. Data may have been revised from previously published statistics to reflect updated information. Executions are not included; for data on executions, see *Capital Punishment, 2009 - Statistical Tables*.

[a] Excludes persons of Hispanic/Latino origin unless specified. bIncludes persons of two or more races or unknown race.

Source: Bureau of Justice Statistics, Deaths in Custody Reporting Program (DCRP).

Table 18. Estimated number of state prisoners in custody at midyear, by selected characteristics, 2001–2009

Characteristic	2001	2002	2003	2004	2005	2006	2007	2008	2009
Total	1,187,800	1,200,000	1,225,700	1,239,700	1,252,500	1,297,300	1,321,800	1,327,100	1,326,600
Sex									
Male	1,110,400	1,121,300	1,143,100	1,155,500	1,165,400	1,205,100	1,227,300	1,232,200	1,232,600
Female	77,500	78,700	82,600	84,200	87,200	92,200	94,500	95,000	94,100
Race/Hispanic origin[a]									
White	425,100	433,800	458,900	453,500	462,800	475,100	479,800	485,800	483,000
Black/African									
American	531,000	524,500	523,500	519,000	517,500	523,300	531,200	536,900	532,700

Characteristic	2001	2002	2003	2004	2005	2006	2007	2008	2009
Hispanic/Latino	160,600	165,900	170,000	180,100	183,300	190,000	196,100	187,000	191,200
American Indian or									
Alaska Native	11,500	12,200	12,600	13,000	13,300	14,300	14,000	14,400	14,700
Asian	5,100	5,400	5,600	5,700	5,900	6,000	6,000	5,500	6,000
Hawaiian or other									
Pacific Islander	2,100	2,100	2,200	2,200	2,100	2,200	2,200	2,400	2,500
Other[b]	8,800	9,500	9,900	10,200	10,400	11,400	12,600	12,400	13,200
Age									
17 or younger	2,900	3,000	2,500	2,500	2,600	2,800	2,700	2,500	2,500
18–24	217,900	216,900	215,800	218,200	220,500	227,600	232,200	189,200	189,100
25–34	403,300	401,000	408,200	412,900	418,400	429,600	440,600	434,000	433,900
35–44	362,900	362,900	364,100	368,200	372,000	384,500	391,800	391,500	391,400
45–54	153,200	163,800	176,500	178,600	180,400	185,600	190,000	232,200	232,100
55 or older	47,900	52,600	57,700	58,300	58,900	60,400	62,000	77,900	77,800

Note: Detail may not sum to total due to missing data. The estimated number of state prisoners presented is rounded. Mortality rates based on this population (tables 19 and 24) are calculated on exact numbers. Data are from the *Prisoners at Midyear* series. Data may have been revised from previously published statistics to reflect updated information. Executions are not included; for data on executions, see *Capital Punishment, 2009 - Statistical Tables*.

[a] Excludes persons of Hispanic/Latino origin unless specified. bIncludes persons of two or more races or unknown race.

Sources: Bureau of Justice Statistics, Deaths in Custody Reporting Program (DCRP), *National Prisoner Statistics* (NPS).

Table 19. Mortality rate per 100,000 state prisoners, by selected characteristics, 2001–2009

Characteristic	2001	2002	2003	2004	2005	2006	2007	2008	2009
Total Sex	242	245	258	252	253	250	257	260	257
Male	250	252	266	259	260	258	265	267	264
Female	129	151	153	162	164	141	145	172	160
Race/Hispanic origin[a]									
White	316	324	348	342	351	343	358	375	366
Black/African American	219	220	230	228	225	220	231	216	225
Hispanic/Latino	202	200	183	184	177	213	196	213	195
American Indian or									
Alaska Native	219	164	193	224	240	175	244	251	212
Asian	78!	225	144!	265	204	135!	185!	327	338
Hawaiian or other									
Pacific Islander	335!	335!	325!	237!	288!	92!	328!	167!	165!
Other[b]	57!	53!	61!	158		132	16!	122	23!

Table 19. (Continued)

Characteristic	2001	2002	2003	2004	2005	2006	2007	2008	2009
Age									
17 or younger	70!	33!	122!	40!		36!	38!	122!	0
18–24	39	29	26	38	35	26	30	35	37
25–34	64	62	68	62	59	58	51	51	48
35–44	181	183	184	168	162	146	131	120	120
45–54	586	555	557	540	560	572	543	458	447
55 or older	2,031	2,007	2,033	2,067	2,102	2,157	2,500	2,092	2,088

Note: Detail may not sum to total due to missing data. Data are from the *Prisoners at Midyear* series. Data may have been revised from previously published statistics to reflect updated information. State prison mortality rates are per 100,000 inmates held in state custody (including private facilities) on June 30th of each year. Prisoner demographic subgroup frequencies are estimated based on the June 30th *National Prisoner Statistics* (NPS) custody counts, demographic data from the National Corrections Reporting Program (NCRP), and the *2004 Survey of Inmates in State Correctional Facilities* (SISCF). The mortality rates presented are calculated on exact population numbers. The mortality rates presented are not adjusted for age, sex, race, geographic location, or any other characteristic. Executions are not included; for data on executions, see *Capital Punishment, 2009 - Statistical Tables*.

! Interpret with caution; too few cases to provide a reliable rate. See *Methodology* for more information.

[a] Excludes persons of Hispanic/Latino origin unless specified.

[b] Includes persons of two or more races or unknown race.

Sources: Bureau of Justice Statistics, Deaths in Custody Reporting Program (DCRP), *National Prisoner Statistics* (NPS) and *2004 Survey of Inmates in State Correctional Facilities* (SISCF).

Table 20. Number of state prisoner deaths, by state, 2001–2009

State	2001	2002	2003	2004	2005	2006	2007	2008	2009
All states[a]	2,877	2,942	3,165	3,129	3,172	3,239	3,392	3,452	3,408
Alabama	87	85	92	65	66	61	54	75	80
Alaska[b]	8	14	4	8	4	6	10	14	7
Arizona	65	74	84	66	78	72	61	77	85
Arkansas	42	31	39	34	38	37	46	41	50
California	288	337	333	348	366	424	395	369	392
Colorado	42	51	47	39	54	31	42	38	49
Connecticut[b]	30	30	36	33	40	25	27	32	29
Delaware[b]	16	15	19	13	19	13	15	15	12
Florida	182	183	221	227	244	261	249	291	278
Georgia	93	105	126	90	122	103	143	128	125
Hawaii[b]	7	13	8	8	8	5	13	14	11

State	2001	2002	2003	2004	2005	2006	2007	2008	2009
Idaho	17	9	12	12	13	18	15	18	13
Illinois	86	72	80	98	72	94	104	71	75
Indiana	47	50	56	56	45	70	54	70	91
Iowa	9	11	13	15	19	12	17	21	14
Kansas	21	22	32	30	19	16	20	24	20
Kentucky	36	41	45	42	43	46	46	69	57
Louisiana	72	78	70	94	89	74	83	117	108
Maine	6	7	2	4	0	6	1	2	4
Maryland	70	71	67	78	57	62	57	69	56
Massachusetts	29	20	30	25	37	39	39	29	29
Michigan	114	113	127	138	140	138	117	99	148
Minnesota	13	15	13	6	13	9	13	17	12
Mississippi	36	33	58	53	63	59	77	54	52
Missouri	57	65	65	77	68	66	78	87	81
Montana	6	5	12	12	12	5	5	9	3
Nebraska	7	8	7	7	8	8	12	6	11
Nevada	27	25	24	31	28	23	39	35	35
New Hampshire	2	9	6	6	8	6	6	5	9
New Jersey	69	60	59	57	61	70	60	66	58
New Mexico	11	15	11	16	18	15	22	30	21
New York	175	185	198	153	170	131	148	133	142
North Carolina	67	60	74	95	69	90	99	117	86
North Dakota	3	1	1	1	1	1	0	0	0
Ohio	115	114	91	126	121	106	123	101	120
Oklahoma	51	64	71	53	75	80	98	88	79
Oregon	24	33	25	34	37	40	36	31	28
Pennsylvania	122	126	147	161	149	124	150	145	165
Rhode Island[b]	3	8	8	7	2	8	9	6	7
South Carolina	71	45	63	50	75	65	72	83	49
South Dakota	4	11	11	5	4	4	8	6	4
Tennessee	51	61	97	71	76	84	73	74	69
Texas	408	396	383	395	351	443	436	469	426
Utah	5	9	10	11	8	7	7	11	17
Vermont[b]	3	3	5	1	6	7	1	3	3
Virginia	71	69	93	86	84	78	103	86	87
Washington	29	30	32	37	45	36	39	35	44
West Virginia	17	8	15	13	10	13	19	19	18
Wisconsin	49	50	41	40	29	45	43	44	42
Wyoming	5	3	2	2	8	3	8	9	7
Federal prisoners	301	335	346	333	388	328	368	399	376

Note: Data may have been revised from previously published statistics to reflect updated information. Executions are not included; for data on executions, see *Capital Punishment, 2009 - Statistical Tables.*

[a] Includes 9 prisoner deaths reported by the District of Columbia in 2001. As of December 30, 2001, sentenced felons from the District of Columbia were the responsibility of the Federal Bureau of Prisons (BOP).

[b] Prisons and jails form one integrated system.

Sources: Bureau of Justice Statistics, Deaths in Custody Reporting Program (DCRP) for state data, *National Prisoner Statistics* (NPS) for federal data through 2006, and personal communication with the Federal Bureau of Prisons (BOP) for federal data after 2006.

Table 21. Mortality rate per 100,000 state prisoners, by state, 2001–2009

State	2001	2002	2003	2004	2005	2006	2007	2008	2009
All states[a]	243	245	258	252	253	250	257	260	257
Alabama	365	318	333	261	257	251	222	302	316
Alaskab	192!	333	90!	179!	87!	123!	195!	369	183 !
Arizona	240	254	275	212	240	202	165	246	274
Arkansas	378	266	343	269	302	293	349	310	377
California	178	213	207	213	223	242	224	218	230
Colorado	247	284	252	198	266	144	187	214	275
Connecticut[b]	167	157	187	175	210	128	135	155	146
Delaware[b]	225	220	280	192	275	183	205	208	174
Florida	253	249	286	277	287	295	268	327	304
Georgia	205	226	268	185	256	200	269	237	253
Hawaii[b]	137!	252	151!	146!	140!	86!	230	412	324 !
Idaho	323	163	214	204	212	278	207	334	248
Illinois	188	167	185	221	161	207	228	155	165
Indiana	242	250	265	256	197	293	215	295	370
Iowa	111!	135!	155	174	221	139	193	240	166
Kansas	246	251	354	327	210	179	225	277	232
Kentucky	313	337	354	336	324	298	301	537	435
Louisiana	369	394	354	480	454	364	398	559	527
Maine	355!	385!	102!	201!	0	296!	47!	92!	197 !
Maryland	293	293	278	328	246	270	249	301	246
Massachusetts	278	199	298	249	364	365	352	256	255
Michigan	236	226	256	284	286	272	231	196	314
Minnesota	208	223	178	77!	155	100!	144	217	136
Mississippi	242	214	365	334	382	360	454	419	433
Missouri	202	218	215	256	219	219	261	290	266
Montana	227!	171!	420	490	451	172!	172!	552!	175 !
Nebraska	181!	200!	169!	173!	186!	176!	269	134!	242 !
Nevada	271	248	236	280	251	185	299	269	275
New Hampshire	86!	363!	242!	247!	326!	216!	205!	173!	316 !
New Jersey	241	208	224	217	231	239	229	261	268
New Mexico	191!	252	179!	252	274	220	337	871	602
New York	252	275	300	236	269	206	232	214	238
North Carolina	211	181	220	270	188	239	256	298	211
North Dakota	296!	87!	88!	82!	74!	72!	0	0	0
Ohio	254	254	200	285	273	226	248	209	245
Oklahoma	232	288	326	235	326	347	415	488	433
Oregon	226	291	210	268	290	306	269	230	203
Pennsylvania	333	321	363	401	363	291	333	323	335

State	2001	2002	2003	2004	2005	2006	2007	2008	2009
Rhode Island[b]	90!	221!	226!	200!	59!	219!	236!	154!	189 !
South Carolina	331	203	270	214	325	284	308	339	201
South Dakota	150!	373!	363!	158!	118!	111!	237!	181!	118 !
Tennessee	290	343	501	365	391	433	377	515	481
Texas	278	268	247	253	224	280	274	335	308
Utah	121!	219!	227!	242!	168!	141!	138!	213!	329
Vermont[b]	216!	146	349!	49!	304!	327!	46!	190!	195 !
Virginia	231	223	299	277	271	251	324	265	280
Washington	189	187	198	218	272	209	214	205	262
West Virginia	489	225!	392	326	252!	304	409	383	360
Wisconsin	246	244	188	181	133	202	188	196	189
Wyoming	329!	191!	126!	115!	407!	148!	399!	735!	454 !
Federal prisoners	220	232	227	208	233	192	211	229	181

Note: Data are from the *Prisoners at Midyear* series. Data may have been revised from previously published statistics to reflect updated information. State prison mortality rates are per 100,000 inmates held in state custody (including private facilities) on June 30th of each year.

Federal prison mortality rates are per 100,000 inmates held in federal custody on December 31st of each year. Deaths in federal prisons are not included in the calculation of rates across all states.

The state-specific population frequencies used in these calculations are the latest available, and may not reflect updates that have been made to the total number of state prison inmates.

Mortality rates between states are not directly comparable because rates are not adjusted for age, sex, race, geographic location, or any other characteristic. Executions are not included; for data on executions, see *Capital Punishment, 2009 - Statistical Tables*.

! Interpret with caution; too few cases to provide a reliable rate. See *Methodology* for more information.

[a] Includes 9 prisoner deaths reported by the District of Columbia in 2001. As of December 31, 2001, sentenced felons from the District of Columbia were the responsibility of the Federal Bureau of Prisons (BOP).

[b] Prisons and jails form one integrated system.

Sources: Bureau of Justice Statistics, Deaths in Custody Reporting Program (DCRP) for state data, *National Prisoner Statistics* (NPS) for federal data through 2006, and personal communication with the Federal Bureau of Prisons (BOP) for federal data after 2006.

Table 22. Number of state prisoner deaths, by cause of death and selected characteristics, 2001–2009

	Illness									
Characteristic	Heart disease	Cancer	Liver disease	AIDS-related	All other illnesses[a]	Suicide	Homicide	Drug/alcohol intoxication	Accident	Other/ unknown
Total	7,368	6,661	2,056	1,468	7,948	1,783	448	360	263	421
Sex										
Male	7,110	6,425	1,992	1,391	7,514	1,697	444	346	253	398
Female	258	236	64	77	434	85	4	14	10	22
Race/Hispanic origin[b]										
White	3,881	3,564	1,081	294	3,845	1,042	208	205	143	194
Black/African American	2,804	2,440	513	998	2,993	375	149	67	79	182
Hispanic/Latino	593	538	404	164	974	295	77	72	32	33
American Indian or Alaska Native	48	54	41	5	64	20	4	11	5	4
Asian	14	23	4	3	27	26	4	2	2	3
Hawaiian or other Pacific Islander	11	10	8	0	7	10	1	0	1	1
Other[c]	13	15	3	3	20	8	4	3	0	2
Age										
17 or younger	0	1	0	0	2	8	1	0	1	0
18–24	69	26	5	14	141	259	58	22	22	15
25–34	365	169	39	194	497	594	123	103	57	53
35–44	1,162	783	332	639	1,362	527	132	132	70	85
45–54	2,099	2,141	1,058	487	2,528	293	92	78	63	115
55 or older	3,671	3,536	622	134	3,411	102	42	25	50	150

Note: Detail may not sum to total due to missing data. Data may have been revised from previously published statistics to reflect updated information. Executions are not included; for data on executions, see *Capital Punishment, 2009 - Statistical Tables*.

[a] In 2007, a high number of cases were missing cause of death information. These cases were classified as all other illnesses.

[b] Excludes persons of Hispanic/Latino origin unless specified. [c]Includes persons of two or more races or unknown race.

Source: Bureau of Justice Statistics, Deaths in Custody Reporting Program (DCRP).

Table 23. Percent of state prisoner deaths, by cause of death and selected characteristics, 2001-2009

	Illness									
Characteristic	Heart disease	Cancer	Liver disease	AIDS related	All other illnessesa	Suicide	Homicide	Drug/alcohol intoxication	Accident	Other/ unknown
Total	100 %	100 %	100 %	100 %	100 %	100 %	100 %	100 %	100 %	100 %
Sex										
Male	96.5 %	96.5 %	96.9 %	94.8 %	94.5 %	95.2 %	99.1 %	96.1 %	96.2 %	94.5 %
Female	3.5	3.5	3.1	5.2	5.5	4.8	0.9	3.9	3.8	5.2
Race/Hispanic originb										
White	52.7 %	53.5 %	52.6 %	20.0 %	48.4 %	58.4 %	46.4 %	56.9 %	54.4 %	46.1 %
Black/ African American	38.1	36.6	25.0	68.0	37.7	21.0	33.3	18.6	30.0	43.2
Hispanic/ Latino	8.0	8.1	19.6	11.2	12.3	16.5	17.2	20.0	12.2	7.8
American Indian or Alaska Native	0.7	0.8	2.0	0.3	0.8	1.1	0.9	3.1	1.9	1.0
Asian	0.2	0.3	0.2	0.2	0.3	1.5	0.9	0.6	0.8	0.7
Hawaiian or other Pacific Islander	0.1	0.2	0.4	0.0	0.1	0.6	0.2	0.0	0.4	0.2
Otherc	0.2	0.2	0.2	0.2	0.4	0.4	0.9	0.8	0.0	0.5
Age										
17 or younger	0.0 %	0.0 %	0.0 %	0.0 %	0.0 %	0.4 %	0.2 %	0.0 %	0.4 %	0.0 %
18–24	0.9	0.4	0.2	1.0	1.8	14.5	12.9	6.1	8.4	3.6
25–34	5.0	2.5	1.9	13.2	6.3	33.3	27.5	28.6	21.7	12.6
35–44	15.8	11.8	16.1	43.5	17.1	29.6	29.5	36.7	26.6	20.2
45–54	28.5	32.1	51.5	33.2	31.8	16.4	20.5	21.7	24.0	27.3
55 or older	49.8	53.1	30.3	9.1	42.9	5.7	9.4	6.9	19.0	35.6

Note: Detail may not sum to total due to missing data. Data may have been revised from previously published statistics to reflect updated information. Executions are not included; for data on executions, see *Capital Punishment, 2009 - Statistical Tables.*

[a] In 2007, a high number of cases were missing cause of death information. These cases were classified as all other illnesses.

[b] Excludes persons of Hispanic/Latino origin unless specified. [c]Includes persons of two or more races or unknown race.

Source: Bureau of Justice Statistics, Deaths in Custody Reporting Program (DCRP).

Table 24. Mortality rate per 100,000 state prisoners, by cause of death and selected characteristics, 2001–2009

	Illness									
Characteristic	Heart disease	Cancer	Liver disease	AIDSrelated	All other illnessesa	Suicide	Homicide	Drug/alcohol intoxication	Accident	Other/ unknown
Total	65	59	18	13	70	16	4	3	2	4
Sex										
Male	67	61	19	13	71	16	4	3	2	4
Female	33	30	8	10	55	11	1!	2	1!	3
Race/Hispanic origin[b]										
White	93	86	26	7	93	25	5	5	3	5
Black/African American	59	52	11	21	63	8	3	1	2	4
Hispanic/Latino	37	33	25	10	60	18	5	4	2	2
American Indian or Alaska Native	40	45	34	4!	54	17	3!	9!	4!	3!
Asian	28	45	8!	6!	53	51	8!	4!	4!	6!
Hawaiian or other Pacific Islander	56!	51!	41!	0	36!	51!	5!	0	5!	5!
Other[c]	13	15	3!	3!	20	8!	4!	3!	0	2!
Age										
17 or younger	0	4!	0	0	9!	34!	4!	0	4!	0
18–24	4	1	--	1	7	13	3	1	1	1
25–34	10	5	1	5	13	16	3	3	2	1
35–44	34	23	10	19	40	16	4	4	2	3
45–54	124	127	63	29	149	17	5	5	4	7
55 or older	664	639	113	24	617	18	8	5	9	27

Note: Detail may not sum to total due to missing data. Data are from the *Prisoners at Midyear* series. Data may have been revised from previously published statistics to reflect updated information. State prison mortality rates are per 100,000 inmates held in state custody (including private facilities) on June 30th of each year. Prisoner demographic subgroup frequencies are estimated based on the June 30th *National Prisoner Statistics* (NPS) custody counts, demographic data from the National Corrections Reporting Program (NCRP), and the *2004 Survey of Inmates in State Correctional Facilities* (SISCF). The mortality rates presented are calculated on exact population numbers. The mortality rates presented are not adjusted for age, sex, race, geographic location, or any other characteristic. Executions are not included; for data on executions, see *Capital Punishment, 2009 - Statistical Tables*.

-- Less than 0.5.

! Interpret with caution; too few cases to provide a reliable rate. See *Methodology* for more information.

[a] In 2007, a high number of cases were missing cause of death information. These cases were classified as all other illnesses.

[b] Excludes persons of Hispanic/Latino origin unless specified.
[c] Includes persons of two or more races or unknown race.
Sources: Bureau of Justice Statistics, Deaths in Custody Reporting Program (DCRP), *National Prisoner Statistics* (NPS) and *2004 Survey of Inmates in State Correctional Facilities* (SISCF).

Table 25. Number of state prisoner deaths, by cause of death and state, 2001–2009

	Illness										
State	All causes	Heart disease	Cancer	Liver disease	AIDS-related	All other illnesses[a]	Suicide	Homicide	Drug/alcohol intoxication	Accident	Other/ unknown
All states[b]	28,776	7,368	6,661	2,056	1,468	7,948	1,783	448	360	263	421
Alabama	665	145	132	45	31	227	10	6	1	7	61
Alaskac	75	14	6	4	0	24	13	2	5	6	1
Arizona	662	150	147	76	19	190	48	11	16	2	3
Arkansas	358	99	77	12	19	109	24	8	1	7	2
California	3,252	460	655	284	106	1,180	285	113	111	23	35
Colorado	393	66	56	51	0	159	30	8	14	9	0
Connecticut[c]	282	66	30	40	4	94	42	2	2	2	0
Delaware[c]	137	25	19	5	17	47	15	2	0	0	7
Florida	2,136	433	579	122	222	645	62	29	5	17	22
Georgia	1,035	348	262	66	66	199	52	21	1	10	10
Hawaii[c]	87	19	16	11	2	20	15	2	0	1	1
Idaho	127	35	36	5	1	29	16	2	0	1	2
Illinois	752	214	201	42	55	147	65	9	6	8	5
Indiana	539	155	108	40	14	145	39	12	12	8	6
Iowa	131	30	45	4	2	32	16	0	0	0	2
Kansas	204	48	50	19	1	64	12	2	2	5	1
Kentucky	425	144	113	22	22	108	11	1	1	2	1
Louisiana	785	195	229	36	78	171	16	4	0	3	53
Maine	32	10	8	3	1	6	2	1	1	0	0
Maryland	587	130	107	22	93	110	48	22	44	4	7
Massachusetts	277	81	59	16	6	69	25	1	9	4	7
Michigan	1,134	411	302	44	33	247	60	6	9	14	8
Minnesota	111	21	30	9	1	32	15	0	2	1	0
Mississippi	485	211	102	18	15	103	20	4	3	8	1
Missouri	644	198	154	67	16	151	36	11	4	5	2
Montana	69	12	17	12	0	16	9	1	1	1	0
Nebraska	74	15	12	8	2	19	3	0	3	1	11
Nevada	267	64	53	14	9	66	17	6	1	2	35
New Hampshire	57	8	17	6	2	14	8	0	2	0	0
New Jersey	560	154	118	25	72	130	30	7	8	5	11

Table 25. (Continued)

	Illness										
State	All causes	Heart disease	Cancer	Liver disease	AIDS-related	All other illnesses[a]	Suicide	Homicide	Drug/alcohol intoxication	Accident	Other/ unknown
New Mexico	159	27	39	15	2	52	15	4	4	1	0
New York	1,435	361	315	69	183	337	107	12	13	18	20
North Carolina	757	193	224	51	44	192	27	8	2	14	2
North Dakota	8	3	1	1	0	2	1	0	0	0	0
Ohio	1,017	327	283	47	27	256	54	12	1	5	5
Oklahoma	659	159	150	68	16	161	32	33	15	9	16
Oregon	288	65	81	29	4	70	21	2	8	4	4
Pennsylvania	1,289	385	301	114	29	368	60	7	6	7	12
Rhode Islandc	58	12	9	1	3	7	13	1	3	3	6
South Carolina	573	227	94	28	28	155	20	16	1	2	2
South Dakota	57	21	5	6	0	12	8	2	0	3	0
Tennessee	656	205	143	39	33	172	28	15	12	4	5
Texas	3,707	951	782	333	119	1,211	224	31	13	25	18
Utah	85	19	8	4	0	24	21	2	3	1	3
Vermontc	31	9	4	6	3	1	5	0	3	0	0
Virginia	757	196	241	56	43	156	28	4	1	3	29
Washington	327	72	86	35	9	91	19	5	3	4	3
West Virginia	132	56	40	2	4	25	3	1	1	0	0
Wisconsin	383	103	109	20	10	82	50	0	4	3	2
Wyoming	47	15	6	3	1	17	3	0	1	1	0
Federal prisoners	3,174	...	...	...	139	2,757	137	73	...	40	28

Note: Detail may not sum to total due to missing data. Data may have been revised from previously published statistics to reflect updated information. Executions are not included; for data on executions, see *Capital Punishment, 2009 - Statistical Tables*.

... Not available. With the exception of AIDS-related deaths, the Federal Bureau of Prisons (BOP) did not break out illness deaths by a specific cause of death (e.g., cancer and liver disease).

[a] In 2007, a high number of cases were missing cause of death information. These cases were classified as all other illnesses.

[b] Includes 9 prisoner deaths reported by the District of Columbia in 2001. As of December 30, 2001, sentenced felons from the District of Columbia were the responsibility of the Federal Bureau of Prisons (BOP).

[c] Prisons and jails form one integrated system.

Sources: Bureau of Justice Statistics, Deaths in Custody Reporting Program (DCRP) for state data, *National Prisoner Statistics* (NPS) for federal data through 2006, and personal communication with the Federal Bureau of Prisons (BOP) for federal data after 2006.

Table 26. Mortality rate per 100,000 state prisoners, by cause of death and state, 2001–2009

	Illness										
State	All causes	Heart disease	Cancer	Liver disease	AIDS- related	All otherillnesses[a]	Suicide	Homicide	Drug/alcohol intoxication	Accident	Other/ unknown
All states[b]	253	65	59	18	13	70	16	4	3	2	4
Alabama	292	64	58	20	14	100	4!	3!	0!	3!	27
Alaska[c]	190	35	15!	10!	0	61	33	5!	13!	15!	3!
Arizona	232	53	51	27	7	67	17	4!	6	1!	1!
Arkansas	321	89	69	11	17	98	21	7!	1!	6!	2!
California	217	31	44	19	7	79	19	8	7	2	2
Colorado	227	38	32	29	0	92	17	5!	8	5!	0
Connecticut[c]	162	38	17	23	2!	54	24	1!	1!	1!	0
Delaware[c]	218	40	30	8!	27	75	24	3!	0	0	11!
Florida	284	58	77	16	30	86	8	4	1!	2	3
Georgia	233	79	59	15	15	45	12	5	0!	2!	2!
Hawaii[c]	193	42	36	24!	4!	44	33	4!	0	2!	2!
Idaho	241	66	68	9!	2!	55	30	4!	0	2!	4!
Illinois	186	53	50	10	14	36	16	2!	1!	2!	1!
Indiana	266	76	53	20	7	72	19	6	6	4!	3!
Iowa	171	39	59	5!	3!	42	21	0	0	0	3!
Kansas	256	60	63	24	1!	80	15	3!	3!	6!	1!
Kentucky	358	121	95	19	19	91	9!	1!	1!	2!	1!
Louisiana	434	108	127	20	43	95	9	2!	0	2!	29
Maine	179	56!	45!	17!	6!	34!	11!	6!	6!	0	0
Maryland	279	62	51	10	44	52	23	10	21	2!	3!
Massachusetts	291	85	62	17	6!	72	26	1!	9!	4!	7!
Michigan	255	92	68	10	7	56	13	1!	2!	3	2!
Minnesota	156	30	42	13!	1!	45	21	0	3!	1!	0
Mississippi	355	154	75	13	11	75	15	3!	2!	6!	1!
Missouri	239	73	57	25	6	56	13	4!	1!	2!	1!
Montana	304	53	75	53	0	71	40!	4!	4!	4!	0
Nebraska	193	39	31	21!	5!	49	8!	0	8!	3!	29!
Nevada	258	62	51	14	9!	64	16	6!	1!	2!	34
New Hampshire	241	34!	72	25!	8!	59	34!	0	8!	0	0
New Jersey	234	64	49	10	30	54	13	3!	3!	2!	5!
New Mexico	311	53	76	29	4	102	29	8!	8!	2!	0
New York	248	62	54	12	32	58	18	2	2	3	3
North Carolina	232	59	69	16	13	59	8	2!	1!	4	1!
North Dakota	70!	26!	9!	9!	0	18!	9!	0	0	0	0
Ohio	244	78	68	11	6	61	13	3	0!	1!	1!
Oklahoma	339	82	77	35	8	83	16	17	8	5!	8
Oregon	255	57	72	26	4!	62	19	2!	7!	4!	4!

Table 26. (Continued)

	Illness										
State	All causes	Heart disease	Cancer	Liver disease	AIDS- related	All otherillnesses[a]	Suicide	Homicide	Drug/alcohol intoxication	Accident	Other/ unknown
Pennsylvania	340	101	79	30	8	97	16	2!	2!	2!	3
Rhode Island[c]	179	37	28!	3!	9!	22!	40	3!	9!	9!	19!
South Carolina	275	109	45	13	13	74	10	8	0!	1!	1!
South Dakota	197	73	17!	21!	0	42	28!	7!	0	10!	0
Tennessee	407	127	89	24	20	107	17	9	7	2!	3!
Texas	273	70	58	25	9	89	16	2	1	2	1
Utah	201	45	19!	9!	0	57	50	5!	7!	2!	7!
Vermont[c]	198	58!	26!	38!	19!	6!	32!	0	19!	0	0
Virginia	269	70	86	20	15	55	10	1!	0!	1!	10
Washington	218	48	57	23	6!	61	13	3!			2!
West Virginia	350	149	106	5!	11!	66	8!	3!	3!	0	0
Wisconsin	196	53	56	10	5!	42	26	0	2!	2!	1!
Wyoming	310	99	40!	20!	7!	112	20!	0	7!	7!	0
Federal prisoners	213	...	...	...	9	185	9	5	...	3	2

Note: Detail may not sum to total due to missing data. Data are from the *Prisoners at Midyear* series. Data may have been revised from previously published statistics to reflect updated information. State prison mortality rates are per 100,000 inmates held in state custody (including private facilities) on June 30th of each year. Federal prison mortality rates are per 100,000 inmates held in federal custody on December 31st of each year. Deaths in federal prisons are not included in the calculation of rates across all states. The state-specific population frequencies used in these calculations are the latest available, and may not reflect updates that have been made to the total number of state prison inmates. The mortality rates presented are not adjusted for age, sex, race, geographic location, or any other characteristic. Executions are not included; for data on executions, see *Capital Punishment, 2009 - Statistical Tables*.

... Not available. With the exception of AIDS-related deaths, the Federal Bureau of Prisons (BOP) did not break out illness deaths by a specific cause of death (e.g., cancer and liver disease).

! Interpret with caution; too few cases to provide a reliable rate. See *Methodology* for more information.

[a] In 2007, a high number of cases were missing cause of death information. These cases were classified as all other illnesses.

[b] Includes 9 prisoner deaths reported by the District of Columbia in 2001. As of December 30, 2001, sentenced felons from the District of Columbia were the responsibility of the Federal Bureau of Prisons (BOP).

[c] Prisons and jails form one integrated system.

Sources: Bureau of Justice Statistics, Deaths in Custody Reporting Program (DCRP) for state data, *National Prisoner Statistics* (NPS) for federal data through 2006, and personal communication with the Federal Bureau of Prisons (BOP) for federal data after 2006.

METHODOLOGY

The Deaths in Custody Reporting Program (DCRP) is an annual data collection conducted by the Bureau of Justice Statistics (BJS). The DCRP collects data on persons who have died while in the custody of the 50 state departments of correction and in the roughly 3,000 local adult jail jurisdictions nationwide.

The DCRP began in 2000 under the Death in Custody Reporting Act of 2000 (P.L. 106-297). It is the only national statistical collection that obtains detailed information about deaths in adult correctional facilities. BJS uses DCRP data to report national trends in the number and causes (or manners) of deaths occurring in state prison or local jail custody.

Information about decedents collected for the DCRP include selected demographic characteristics, such as sex, age, race, and Hispanic ethnicity; facility type of death (prison or jail); date of admission; conviction status; admission offense; circumstances surrounding the death, including cause of death, time and location of death; and information on whether an autopsy was conducted and the availability of results to the respondent. In cases of illness deaths, the DCRP collects data on whether the decedent had a preexisting condition and whether he or she received medical treatment for this condition prior to death.

Executions are collected under the separate BJS *Capital Punishment* series. Data on executions are accessible through the BJS website at www.bjs.gov.

Statistics presented in this report are current as of September 1, 2011. DCRP mortality data are accessible on the BJS website.

For more information on mortality in correctional settings, see *Mortality in Local Jails, 2000-2007* (NCJ 222988, BJS Web, July 2010); *Medical Causes of Death in State Prisons, 2001-2004* (NCJ 216340, BJS Web, January 2007); and *Suicide and Homicide in State Prisons and Local Jails* (NCJ 210036, BJS Web, August 2005).

Scope of the DCRP

The prison component of the DCRP collects data on inmate deaths occurring in the 50 state departments of corrections while inmates are in the physical custody of prison officials. Starting in 2001 and annually thereafter, BJS has collected DCRP data directly from state prison systems. Since beginning the collection, BJS has maintained a 100% response rate from the state prison system respondents to the DCRP.

The DCRP's jail component includes inmate deaths occurring in all local adult jail jurisdictions nationwide. A jail jurisdiction is a legal entity that has responsibility for managing jail facilities. Jail jurisdictions typically operate at the county level, in which a sheriff or executive manages the local facilities. The DCRP data identify the facilities in which a jail death occurs, but the DCRP data are arrayed at the jail jurisdiction level. BJS defines a jail as locally-operated correctional facility that confines persons before or after adjudication for more than 72 hours. BJS does not include temporary lockups in its definition of jail facilities. Typically, there is one facility per jail jurisdiction, but the *2006 Census of Jail Facilities* found that 15% of jail jurisdictions had multiple facilities under its authority. See the BJS website for more information.

The jail universe file includes all currently operating jails as well as jails that have closed, consolidated, or otherwise eliminated operations. The most recent jail universe, constructed in 2009, identified 2,825 jurisdictions, representing 3,223 jail facilities. Of these, 2,755 (97.5%) participated in the 2009 DCRP.

Administration of the DCRP

The DCRP collection forms are provided annually to state prison and local jail respondents. Respondents provide an aggregate count of the number of deaths occurring during the referenced calendar year, in addition to individual-level decedent data. For state prison system respondents, aggregate counts are obtained through the NPS-4 (available at http://bjs.gov/content/pub/pdf/nps410.pdf). For local jails, aggregate counts of deaths are obtained through the CJ-9A (available at http://bjs.gov/content/pub/pdf/cj9a10.pdf).

BJS requests jail administrators to provide statistics about their population and bookings through the summary form in addition to a death count. All jails, even those with no deaths to report, a scenario that applies to about 80% of jails in any given year, are asked to complete the annual summary form.

BJS obtains a separate report describing the decedent's characteristics and the circumstances surrounding the death for each death occurring in a state prison or local jail. The survey forms used to obtain data on each prison and jail death are available on the BJS website:

- Prison deaths (NPS-4A form): http://bjs.gov/content/pub/pdf/nps4a10.pdf
- Jail deaths (CJ-9): http://bjs.gov/content/pub/pdf/cj910.pdf

State prison and local jail respondents may submit individual records on decedents at any time during a collection cycle through a BJS web-based collection system, accessible on the BJS website at https://bjsdcrp.rti.org/.

BJS has modified the survey forms slightly over time. Most of the changes have been minor and intended to clarify existing questions and ease respondent burden.

In 2001, additional items on medical treatment in prisons and jails were added to collect data on medical treatment received by the inmate prior to death. Text boxes added to the forms in 2008 allowed respondents to elaborate on deaths due to intoxication, suicide, and inmate-involved homicide. Such fields had previously only been available for deaths due to illness, accident, homicide not caused by other inmates, and other unspecified reasons. BJS removed a question measuring the conviction status of an inmate (since more than 99% of prison inmates were convicted at the time of their deaths). BJS also changed the survey layout in 2009 to simplify the progression through questions related to autopsies. The revised item instructed respondents to complete the entire form after autopsy results were available (rather than submitting an initially-incomplete form where autopsy results were pending).

Determining Eligibility for Reporting to the DCRP

In the DCRP, custody refers to the holding of an inmate in a facility or while a correctional authority maintains a chain of custody over an inmate. For instance, if a jail transports an ill inmate to a hospital for medical services and that inmate dies while in the chain of custody of the jail, that death is counted as a death in the DCRP. A death that occurs when an inmate is not in the custody of correctional authority is considered to be beyond the scope of the DCRP. This includes deaths of inmates on escape status and those serving time on community corrections (probation, parole, or home-electronic monitoring). Legal executions are also beyond the scope of the DCRP. For more information on executions, see the *Capital Punishment* series on the BJS website.

BJS instructs both state prison and local jail officials to determine first whether the inmate was in the physical custody of the jurisdiction at the time of death, regardless of the reason an inmate was being held. For state prisons, this includes the deaths of inmates held in any private prison facility under contract to the department of corrections as well as deaths in any of their state-operated facilities, including halfway houses, prison camps or farms, training or treatment centers, and prison hospitals.

BJS instructs state prison officials to exclude deaths of inmates who were transferred to local jails due to overcrowding or other reasons but who were still serving a prison term. The DCRP obtains information about these deaths through the jail reports. For jails, deaths in custody includes deaths of inmates who were temporarily out of the physical custody of a facility but within the chain of custody of the jail. Typically, these include deaths of jail inmates who have been transferred to offsite facilities that care for critically-ill persons. Over half (51%) of jail inmate deaths occurred in medical facilities outside of the jail facility between 2000 and 2009.

Custody is further complicated by the dual law enforcement and jail administration functions of some sheriffs' departments. As a result, some deaths reported as jail deaths actually occurred before the jail had custody of the decedent. BJS excludes these deaths in the process of arrest by using information about the circumstances surrounding the death.

Identifying and Excluding Duplicates

Duplicate death records may exist in DCRP due to overlapping correctional populations as well as overlapping duties within correctional facilities. For example, a jail jurisdiction may have more than one reporting unit responsible for reporting data to BJS, or a jail may be holding a state prison inmate. Multiple reporting entities may report the same death, or state prison systems may report on the death of an inmate who was transferred to a local jail but was serving a prison sentence at the time.

BJS' process for identifying duplicate death records is as follows: First, BJS reconciles the aggregate summary counts of deaths occurring during a calendar year with the number of individual death records obtained from a reporting jurisdiction. When BJS identifies discrepancies, it contacts reporting jurisdictions for clarification. Second, BJS performs record-matching to identify duplicate records within jurisdictions. The matching is based on inmate name and date of birth, date of death, and date of admission to the facility. BJS' review of death records between 2000 and 2009 found 83 jail and 294 prison deaths to be duplicates or beyond the scope of DCRP. These records were excluded from all DCRP analyses.

Cause of Death Information

BJS aims to collect accurate information about the cause of death. The instructions for completing the DCRP tell respondents to report death information as determined by an autopsy or other official medical death investigation. Death by intoxication, accident, suicide, and homicide are considered discrete causes of death. While there is a distinction between manner and cause of death from a medico-legal standpoint, no such distinction is made in the DCRP. When reporting deaths due to accident or homicide, BJS requests respondents to describe the events surrounding these deaths. BJS added a text field to the survey forms so that respondents could provide more detailed information on suicide and intoxication deaths. See *Administration of the DCRP*.

Due to the variation in deaths caused by illness, respondents report the cause of death as determined by an autopsy. These causes are later converted by clinical data specialists into standard medical codes according to the World Health Organization's *International Statistical Classification of Diseases and Related Health Problems, Tenth Revision* (ICD-10).

Other BJS Sources of Correctional Mortality Data

BJS maintains other data collections on correctional mortality and deaths in the process of arrest. These other collections include—

- *Capital Punishment*, which provides data on legal executions. (See the BJS website for further discussion of executions.)
- The *National Prisoner Statistics* (NPS), which prior to the establishment of the DCRP, annually collected aggregate counts of deaths in state and federal prisons. Prior to 2007, the NPS collected aggregate counts of deaths occurring in state and federal prisons, and counts of deaths by broad categories of death, specifically deaths due to execution, illness, AIDS, suicide, accident, homicide, and other causes. After 2007, the Federal Bureau of Prisons (BOP) continued to submit the counts of deaths for these broad categories while state

prison officials no longer provided counts of deaths via the NPS. (See the BJS website for further discussion of the NPS.)

- The *Census of Jail Inmates*, which is conducted every five to six years and provides counts of inmate deaths in local jails. (See the BJS website for further discussion of the *Census of Jail Inmates*).
- The *Survey of Jails in Indian Country* (SJIC), which provides aggregate counts of the number of deaths occurring in Indian country correctional facilities operated by tribal authorities or the U.S. Department of Interior's Bureau of Indian Affairs. (See the BJS website for further discussion of the SJIC.)
- *Arrest-Related Deaths* (ARD), which obtains data on deaths occurring during the process of arrest. BJS relies on state-level respondents to provide details of deaths occurring during arrest. (See the BJS website for further discussion of ARD.)

Reported Statistics

Mortality rates are calculated per 100,000 inmates where the denominators provide estimates of the number of person-years of exposure in custody in institutional corrections. The mortality rate for state prisons is calculated as the number of deaths per year divided by the midyear state prison population in custody multiplied by 100,000. Midyear custody counts for state prisons provide estimates for person-years for prison populations. BJS uses data from its *National Prisoner Statistics* (NPS) collection to provide midyear custody counts of prisoners. For more information on the NPS, see the BJS website.

The mortality rate in local jails is calculated as the number of deaths per year divided by the average daily jail inmate population (ADP) multiplied by 100,000. The ADP for local jails is defined as the average daily number of jail inmates held in a jail jurisdiction during a calendar year. The use of the ADP as the denominator for jail mortality rates is based on the high turnover and daily fluctuation in local jail populations. The ADP better reflects the number of inmate days per year than does any one day count.

The jail ADP also reflects the annual number of admissions and mean length of stay, and can be expressed as the product of these two values. When mean length of stay is expressed in years, the ADP is equivalent to the number of person-years spent by jail inmates during a given year. Starting in 2002, BJS collected the ADP directly from respondents using the summary form, CJ-9. Prior to 2002, BJS calculated the jail ADP by taking the average of the

January 1st count and the December 31st count from the reference year, which is a proxy measure for ADP.

Both denominators provide data for annualizing mortality rates, which are calculated separately for each key statistic, by group or by characteristic. The annualized mortality rates by cause of death in state prisons and local jails are comparable to annual crude mortality rates reported by the National Center for Health Statistics (NCHS). NCHS calculates crude mortality rates as the number of events for a period (e.g., year) divided by the population estimate at the midpoint of the period. For general population mortality statistics, NCHS employs the midyear population as an approximation to the average population exposed to risk of death during any given year. (For more information, see Siegal, J. & Swanson, D. (2004), *The Methods and Materials of Demography, Second Edition,* San Diego, CA: Elsevier Academic Press, p. 269.)

The crude mortality rates reported in the DCRP annual statistical tables for particular segments of the incarcerated population are not directly comparable to the crude mortality rates within the (non-incarcerated) general population. In addition, the crude mortality rates in state prisons are not directly comparable to those of local jails. Since the age, race, and sex composition of the general population differs from that in state prisons and local jails, and since mortality is correlated with age, race, and sex, the crude mortality rates in state prisons and local jails should not be compared directly to one another, or to the general population.

Estimating Inmate Population Characteristics for Use in Calculating Mortality Rates by Demographic Subgroups

BJS does not obtain annual data for all demographic characteristics of prison and jail inmates in all jurisdictions. BJS uses data from sources other than the DCRP to estimate the nationwide age, race, and sex composition of state prison and local jail inmate populations. These data sources consist primarily of periodic surveys of inmates in custody in prisons and jails. The inmate characteristic distributions obtained from these surveys are applied to denominators (counts of inmates or ADP) to estimate the number of inmates in each demographic subgroup.

BJS estimated the demographic distribution of the state prison population data from the *National Prisoner Statistics* (NPS) and National Corrections Reporting Program (NCRP) collections. For a discussion on the methodology for obtaining estimates of the age, race, and sex distributions of state prisoners, see *Prisoners in 2009* (NCJ 231675, BJS web, December 2010).

Prior BJS reports of mortality rates for state prison inmates used demographic distributions derived from BJS' *2004 Survey of Inmates in State and Federal Correctional Facilities* (SISCF). Consequently, the state prison mortality rates shown in these tables may differ from previously published rates. A rate comparison between the two sources showed very little difference in the resultant mortality rates. In most instances, the rates either matched or nearly matched.

To estimate the distributions of demographic attributes of the ADP for local jail inmates, BJS used data from several surveys to generate distributions of age, race, and sex, and applied these distributions to the ADP. BJS' *Annual Survey of Jails* (ASJ) provided estimates of the race, ethnic, and sex distribution of local jail inmates for each year of the DCRP collection and applied these to each year's ADP from the DCRP to estimate the average daily population of persons in these demographic categories. For more information on the ASJ, see *Jail Inmates at Midyear 2010 - Statistical Tables* (NCJ 233431, BJS Web, April 2011).

Unlike sex and race/ethnicity data, BJS does not annually collect data on age in jail populations. BJS obtained estimates of the age distribution of jail inmates from the *2002 Survey of Inmates in Local Jails* (SILJ) and the 2007 and 2008-09 *National Inmate Survey* (NIS) available on the BJS website. For more information about jail inmates, see *Profile of Jail Inmates, 2002* (NCJ 201932, BJS Web, July 2004).

To estimate the age distribution of the jail inmate population, we first obtained an estimate of the number of

jail inmates under age 18 from the *Annual Survey of Jails* (ASJ). Between 2000 and 2010, the number of jail inmates under age 18 has ranged between 6,100 and 7,615, according to *Jail Inmates at Midyear 2010* (table 6). By applying the annual percentage of jail inmates under age 18 to the annual average daily jail inmate population, we estimated the average daily population of jail inmates under age 18.

To estimate the age distribution of adult jail inmates, BJS used data from the *Survey of Inmates in Local Jails* (SILJ) and the *National Inmate Survey* (NIS). We used the SILJ estimates to cover the period from 2000 to 2006 and the NIS estimates to cover the period from 2007 to 2009. In each case, we applied the percentages associated with each age category to the adults in jail average daily population.

Random Error and Suppression

The DCRP data on deaths in state prisons and local jails are not subject to sampling error. However, mortality data from a complete or near complete enumeration may be subject to random error. Following Brillinger and NCHS, "the number of deaths that actually occurred may be considered as one of a large series of possible results that could have arisen under the same set of circumstances" (NCHS, 2007). The random variation can be large when the number of deaths is small; hence, considerable caution is warranted when interpreting statistics based on small numbers of deaths. According to NCHS standards, mortality rates based on fewer than 100 deaths per year should be interpreted with caution. For more information on vital rates, see Brillinger, D. R. (1986), "The natural variability of vital rates and associated statistics," *Biometrics* 42:693-734. See also the *National Vital Statistics Reports. Deaths: Final Data for 2007*, Centers for Disease Control and Prevention, National Center for Health Statistics, retrieved from http://www.cdc.gov/nchs/data/nvsr/nvsr58/nvsr58_19.pdf.

Further following NCHS and Brillinger, we quantify random variation by assuming that the appropriate underlying distribution is a Poisson probability distribution. This provides for a computationally simple as well as reasonable approach to estimate variances for mortality statistics when the probability of dying is low. We calculated variances based on the assumption of a Poisson process and from these variances calculated relative random error estimates, which are comparable to relative standard error, in that the relative random error is the ratio of random error derived from the Poisson variance to the number of deaths. Following NCHS, when the relative random error exceeded 30%, we flagged estimated mortality rates due to the instability of the rate.

Survey Performance Issues

Survey administration and modifications to the survey form generated data for years 2007 through 2009 that may not be wholly compatible with prior DCRP data. In 2007, state prison officials categorized a large number of illness deaths as all other illnesses, which led to a high degree of missing data on illness causes of death. In 2008, local jail officials were unable to provide causes of death for 22% of jail inmate deaths. During 2009, BJS made modifications to the collection instruments to improve reporting and reduce burden.

- **Item nonresponse in 2007:** The number of illness deaths categorized as all other illnesses was overstated in the 2007 prison death reports. This arose from a high degree of item nonresponse in the text box requesting specific illness designation on the prisoner death form (NPS-4A). Since the "all other illnesses" category included unknown or unspecified illnesses, we were able to classify deaths within this broad category into specific causes when respondents reported an illness death and the additional cause of death information. Throughout the DCRP prison collection, state departments of corrections respondents were unable to provide more detailed information on an average of 17 illness deaths per year between 2001 and 2006. During 2007, this frequency increased to 173 deaths. Since many of these deaths would likely have been classified in the most common illness categories (e.g., heart disease, cancer, or liver disease), the number of known illness deaths was low in 2007 relative to prior years. The distribution of illness deaths in state prisons during 2007 reflect only the deaths for which specific illness determinations could be made.
- **Item nonresponse in 2008 jail data and unknown cause of death:** An abnormally large number of cases were missing a response for cause of death in the 2008 jail file (n=209; 21.8% of all jail deaths in 2008). This coincided with the final year the U.S. Census Bureau acted as the data collection agent for DCRP. In prior years of the DCRP jail data collection, an average of 6% of all deaths were classified as having other or unknown causes of death. For the purposes of this report, BJS categorized the cause of death for these 209 jail deaths from 2008 as other/unknown.
- **2009 data collection:** Prior to the 2009 DCRP collection, BJS reviewed the data collection instrument, data submission procedures, and assessed the communications with DCRP respondents with the goal to reduce burden on respondents. This resulted in modifications to the survey instrument to facilitate the online data collection tool to encourage online response. These modifications led to delays in implementing the collection. As a result, individual death reports were collected retrospectively for the first time, rather than in the year the death occurred.

INDEX

D

E

F

M

N

O

P

Q

R

S